Dear MyCopy Customer,

This Springer book is a monochrome print version of the eBook to which your library gives you access via SpringerLink. It is available to you at a subsidized price since your library subscribes to at least one Springer eBook subject collection.

Please note that MyCopy books are only offered to library patrons with access to at least one Springer eBook subject collection. MyCopy books are strictly for individual use only.

You may cite this book by referencing the bibliographic data and/or the DOI (Digital Object Identifier) found in the front matter. This book is an exact but monochrome copy of the print version of the eBook on SpringerLink.

SCORING PERFORMANCE ASSESSMENTS BASED ON JUDGEMENTS

Generalizability Theory

Evaluation in Education and Human Services

Editors:

George F. Madaus, Boston College, Chestnut Hill, Massachusetts, U.S.A.

Daniel L. Stufflebeam, Western Michigan University, Kalamazoo, Michigan, U.S.A.

Other books in the series:

Gable, R.E.:
Instrument Development in the Affective Domain (2nd Edition)
Kremer-Hayon, L.:
Teacher Self-Evaluation
Payne, David A.:
Designing Educational Project and Program Evaluations
Oakland T. and Hambleton, R.:
International Perspectives on Academic Assessment
Nettles, M.T. and Nettles, A.L.:
Equity and Excellence in Educational Testing and Assessment
Shinkfield, A.J. and Stufflebeam, D.L.:
Teacher Evaluation: Guide to Effective Practice
Birenbaum, M. and Dochy, Filip J.R.C.:
Alternatives in Assessment of Achievements, Learning Processes and Prior Knowledge
Mulder, M., Nijhof, W.J., Brinkerhoff, R.O.:
Corporate Training for Effective Performance
Britton, E.D. and Raizen, S.A.:
Examining the Examinations
Candoli, C., Cullen, K. and Stufflebeam, D.:
Superintendent Performance Evaluation
Brown, S.M. and Seidner, C.J.:
Evaluating Corporate Training: Models and Issues
Osterlind, S.:
Constructing Test Items (Second Edition)
Nettles, M.T. and Nettles, A.L.:
Challenges Minorities Face in Educational Testing and Assessment
Stufflebeam, D.L., Madaus, G.F. and Kellaghan, T.:
Evaluation Models: Viewpoints on Educational and Human Services Evaluation (Second Edition)

SCORING PERFORMANCE ASSESSMENTS BASED ON JUDGEMENTS
Generalizability Theory

by

Christopher Wing-Tat Chiu
University of Pittsburgh

Springer Science+Business Media, LLC

Library of Congress Cataloging-in-Publication Data

A C.I.P. Catalogue record for this book is available
from the Library of Congress.

DOI 10.1007/978-94-010-0650-7

Printed on acid-free paper.

springer.com/mycopy

To Ivy,

Sue, Stella, Kenneth, Grace,

Siu Wai, Lai Ping, my grandparents, and

the great minds in measurement

CONTENTS

LIST OF FIGURES

LIST OF TABLES

LIST OF APPENDICES

PREFACE

In generalizability analyses, unstable and potentially invalid variance component estimates may result from using only a limited portion of available data. However, missing observations are common in operational performance assessment settings (e.g., Brennan, 1992 and 1997; Cronbach, Gleser, Nanda, & Rajaratnam, 1972; Shavelson & Webb, 1991) because of the nature of the assessment design. This book describes a procedure to analyze data with missing observations by extracting data from a sparsely-filled data matrix into analyzable smaller subsets of data. This subdividing method (Chiu & Wolfe, in press), drawing on the conceptual framework in meta-analysis (e.g., Hedges & Olkin, 1985), is accomplished by creating data sets that exhibit structural designs (i.e., *crossed*, *nested*, and *modified balanced incomplete block* designs) then pooling variance components obtained from these designs. This method is always more computationally effective than any other methods that require sparsely collected scores to be analyzed all at once. A Monte Carlo simulation is used to examine the statistical properties of the variance-component estimates and some commonly used composite indices, namely the generalizability coefficient (for norm-referenced decisions), the dependability coefficient (for criterion-referenced decisions), and the misclassification rates. The smallest unbalanced data set used to evaluate the subdividing method is composed of 750 examinees, four raters, and two tasks while the largest unbalanced data subset is composed of 6000 examinees, 28 raters, and two tasks. Graphic displays are used to evaluate the accuracy, stability, and consistency of the variance component estimates and the composite indices. Experimental conditions, modeling operational performance assessments, are manipulated to examine how well the subdividing method would perform in practice. These conditions included: (1) volume of examinees, (2) size of rater pool, (3) variation in item difficulty, (4) levels of rater inconsistency, (5) rules used to decide how to group raters and assign tasks to raters, and (6) the minimum number of examinees scored by a group of raters.

Results indicate that the subdividing method produce outcomes having properties (unbaisedness and consistency) that are similar to those of complete data methods. Evidence was provided to support that the pattern of missing data was frequently, in large-scale performance assessments, determined by the rules used to assign examinees and tasks to raters during scoring sessions. A collection of these rules, defined as a *rating plan*, was examined. Specifically, this book compared two prevalent rating plans (i.e., the *disconnected crossed* and *connected mixture* plans). It was found that increasing the number of raters to score examinees boosts the precision in estimating rater-related measurement errors, namely *rater-* and *rater-by-item* errors, for the *disconnected crossed* rating plan but lowers the precision for the *connected mixture* rating plan in the universe of generalization utilizing a $p \times I \times R$ design.

The subdividing method recovers variance component estimates with high accuracy and precision in a variety of conditions (i.e., low and high variations in item difficulty and rater inconsistency). Increasing the number of examinees scored by groups of raters from 12 to 24 has virtually no effect on the accuracy and precision of the variance component estimates. This book also illustrates that: (1) the amounts and patterns of missing data influence the standard error to a larger degree than they influence the accuracy of the variance component estimates, assuming unobserved scores are missing completely at random, and (2) the use of only a few tasks varying much in difficulty is a major source of variation, which lowers the dependability of measurement procedures and thus leading to unreliable criterion-reference decisions. It is evident that the subdividing method can detect this major source of variation in performance assessments.

Computer programs are developed to automate and validate the Subdividing method. Not only can these programs be used in the current research, but also they can be used in other large-scale simulation projects requiring the use of multiple computers. Also, a rater profiling system is delineated for tracking the process by which massive amounts of responses are distributed to raters in large-scale assessments. The profiling system can be used in designing cost-effective rater plans. It also serves as a means to monitor the reliability of test scores assigned by a large group of raters where score comparisons cannot be made in a straightforward manner.

ACKNOWLEDGMENTS

Many have supported this book throughout the years. The University of Pittsburgh, the Society of Multivariate Experimental Psychology (SMEP), Michigan State University, the Educational Testing Service (ETS), and the American College Testing Program (ACT) provided generous support through their fellowships and grant programs.

I am in debt to Robert Floden, Betsy Becker, William Mehrens, and David Pearson; and my colleagues and friends, Isaac Bejar and Edward Wolfe. My early interest in the Generalizability theory and performance assessment was fostered in a seminar led by Robert Floden and David Pearson. The invaluable feedback and kind support provided by Betsy Becker, the SynRG meta-analysis research group, and the faculty of the Measurement and Quantitative Method program at Michigan State University are deeply appreciated. Betsy Becker's editing skills taught me the importance of being thorough to produce high quality work. Robert Floden's keen research skills and high standards helped me focus and expand my thinking. I would like to thank William Mehrens for his inspiring teaching in psychometrics and educational measurement. My mentor, Edward Wolfe stimulated my thoughts for this research monograph, while I participated in a summer internship at ACT in 1996.

Isaac Bejar, my mentor at ETS while I was a pre-doctoral fellow, gave me ample opportunities to master technical skills indispensable for the completion of this book. The simulation in this book would not have been possible without the equipment sponsored by ETS, the University of Pittsburgh, and Michigan State University. Many thanks to Carol Baker, Robert Brennan, Randy Fotiu, Brad Hanson, Michael Harewell, Cholyeun Hongpaisanwiwat, Suzanne Lane, Mark MacCullen, Eiji Muraki, George Novacky, Neil Timm, Paul Nichols, Connie Page, Mark Reckase, Philip Smith, Jon Sticklen, Clement Stone, Ross Traub, and Louis Trentini who shared their extensive knowledge and provided me with their insights in research methods and knowledge in software development employed in this book.

I thank my best friend and significant other, Ivy Li, for believing in me and provided me with endless support and laughter. I also want to thank her for all her help in editing the monograph and for her many ideas. Last but not least, I would like to express my deepest gratitude to my family for their understanding and encouragement; I am grateful to my parents, Siu-Wai and Lai-Ping, and Aunts Sue and Grace for everything they have taught me.

This book is inspired by Robert Floden, Robert Brennan and Lee Cronbach. The opinions expressed in this book are mine, and do not necessarily reflect the views of the Kluwer Academic Publisher, University of Pittsburgh, ACT, Inc., and ETS. I have benefited from the advice of many individuals, but any errors in this book remain mine.

Chapter 1
INTRODUCTION

The importance of Generalizability theory (G theory) lies in its applications to educational measurement. Two of its major functions are: 1) to evaluate the quality of measurement procedures; and 2) to make projections about how one can improve the quality of measurement procedures. Regardless of its wide applications (Brennan, 1997, 1998; Lane, Ankenmann, & Stone, 1996; and Linn, Burton, DeStefano, & Hanson, 1996), G theory, a framework relying on the estimation of variance components, has a major limitation in its capability of handling missing data — a common problem in large-scale assessments. Test developers often cannot use ordinary algorithms for estimating variance components in G theory because of the excessive computational requirements.

The current research monograph developed and scrutinized a method called the subdividing method (defined in Chapter 3), which allows investigators to use more of the data, with lower computational power needs than conventional methods. It also examines the subdividing method as a way to obtain G theory estimates for large-scale assessments by exploring the robustness of this method across a variety of experimental conditions reflecting realistic operational processes adopted by performance assessment centers. Specifically, the current study examines the accuracy and precision (defined in the chapter 3 entitled "Methodology") of the estimators recovered by the subdividing method. "Literature Review" in chapter 2 summarizes and critiques conventional methods used for analyzing missing data with a focus on those applied to G theory. Chapter 2 also summarizes the background of the research questions, which are stated in detail in chapter 3. Along with the research questions, chapter 3 describes the three major steps to implement the subdividing method, namely "Subdividing", "Estimating", and "Synthesizing". In addition, that chapter also reveals the experimental conditions manipulated to evaluate the subdividing method. Chapter 3 also discusses technical issues in applying the subdividing method and practical issues in planning scoring sessions for open-ended questions.

Questions regarding the planning of scoring procedures include: In what way should test developers set up a scoring procedure? How does the use of different set-ups influence the quality of quantifying measurement errors? How many examinees and tasks should a common group of raters score in order to obtain a reliable scoring procedure? Technical questions regarding the subdividing method include: What are the situations in which one can ignore weighting schemes when synthesizing data subsets? What are the consequences of not using weights? When does one need to use weights? To what extent can the subdividing method produce accurate and precise G theory estimates for large volumes of examinees and raters? How sensitive is the subdividing method in estimating reliability when measurement errors are small and when they are large? Chapter 4 reports the results, which are all in the context of data missing completely at random (MCAR, Little & Rubin, 1987). Chapter 5 summarizes the results, which are interpreted in the light of providing suggestions to test developers. The last chapter delineates three Windows®-based computer programs to implement the subdividing method and to conduct large-scale simulation research. Chapter 6 also discusses a coding system to profile the process to distribute essays to raters (denoted "rater design"). Both the computer programs and the rater profiling system have applications in addition to the research described in this book.

1.1 SIGNIFICANCE OF THE CURRENT STUDY

Currently, researchers are frequently forced to discard data when some data are missing, leading to unstable variance components and reliability coefficient estimates used to evaluate measurement procedures in large-scale assessments. Interpreting those unstable estimates can lead to inconsistent decisions (Burdick 1992, pp.16-18). For example, if our goal is to develop a performance assessment procedure with a generalizability coefficient of 0.90, we may reach different conclusions using the following three confidence intervals [0.85, 0.89], [0.44, 0.89], and [0.44, 0.50]. In the first case, we may conclude that for practical purposes, the generalizability coefficient is close enough to 0.90 that it may not be efficient to increase the reliability. In the second case, we may decide that the confidence interval is too wide to make conclusive decisions about the reliability of the assessment procedure. In the final scenario, the evidence suggests that the assessment procedure is not well developed. In the context of scoring performance tasks in which observations and judgements are involved, the final scenario indicates that raters differ greatly in severity and need further training. The current book evaluates the subdividing method in terms of point estimates, standard errors, and confidence intervals of the variance components and composite indices.

The amount of missing data and the mechanism causing data to be missing are nontrivial factors, because they affect standard errors of the estimates (Little & Rubin, 1987). When generalizability coefficients have sizable sampling errors, scores are also unreliable and decision makers may assign a higher rank to one examinee than to other examinees on one occasion but not on other occasions. Like generalizability-coefficient estimates, variance-component estimates are not as precise when observed data are discarded in dealing with incomplete data. By reducing the amount of data to be discarded, the proposed subdividing method produces more stable decision study results (Cronbach et al., 1972).

Another limitation of G theory is that it demands intensive computational resources to model unbalanced data (Babb, 1986; Bell, 1985; Brennan, 1992; Brennan, 1997; Searle, 1992; Shavelson, 1981). Estimation methods for G theory often require extensive computational resources. Methods like Restricted Maximum Likelihood require large amounts of computational resources to analyze data matrices that can be too large to invert. For example, Bell (1985) analyzed a survey containing the responses of 831 students from 112 schools with each student answering 11 questions (each response constituting a separate record so the total number of records were $11 \times 831 = 9141$). Bell compared the processing time of two procedures for estimating variance components using the SAS system (SAS Institute, Inc., 1985), namely the VARCOMP procedure (i.e., TYPE1 and ML) and the GLM procedure. In all cases, a minimum of five minutes of central processing unit time was needed to complete the estimation procedure. We had a similar experience with the data analyzed for this study (5905 x 2 x 9 cells). At one point in our preliminary analyses of the data presented in this article, we allowed the SAS VARCOMP procedure to run for over 24 hours on a UNIX RS6000 computer, and the estimation procedures still did not converge. To overcome the large-scale problem, the subdividing method reduces the intensive computational demands by partitioning a large unbalanced data set into smaller data subsets.

Data collection procedures determine the pattern of missing data (Engelhard, 1997) and thus influence the precision of parameter estimates (Little & Rubin, 1987). In multiple facet generalizability studies employed for large-scale assessments, the ways to assign tasks to raters and the mechanisms to distribute examinees' work to raters constitute the data collection procedures, also defined as "rating plans" throughout the current monograph. Although data collection procedures are critical, rarely did research set out to investigate how these procedures influence the statistical properties of G theory estimates (Personal communication from Gordon, 1998; Vickers, 1998;

& Welch, 1996). The current monograph summarizes two data collection procedures frequently appeared in the literature for scoring open-ended questions based on human judgements. It then deduces principles underlying these procedures. The robustness and performance of the proposed subdividing method is evaluated, utilizing a Monte Carlo simulation, in operational settings parallel to the two data collection procedures.

Existing research relevant to G theory for unbalanced data has tended to focus on the estimation of variance components outside of the measurement framework. In particular, much research (e.g., Babb, 1986; Burdick, 1992; Henderson, 1953; Malley, 1986; Marcoulides, 1988; Rao, 1997; Satterthwaite, 1946; Searle, 1992; Seeger, 1970; Townsend, 1968) has focused on the statistical properties of variance components. No research has examined the statistical properties for composite indices commonly used in G theory, particularly in unbalanced situations. The current monograph compensates for this demerit. Knowing the statistical properties for variance components alone does not necessarily help us to interpret composite indices. Nor does it help us to make decisions regarding the reliability of a measurement procedure. (For the applications of the composite indices, see the subsequent section entitled *Indices Commonly Used in Criterion-Referenced and Norm-Referenced Tests*.) For instance, knowing the confidence intervals for the variance components, per se, does not allow inferences to the confidence intervals for the standard errors of measurement and for the dependability coefficient. This is because the variance components do not have a linear relationship with all the composite indices (e.g., the absolute standard error of measurement is the square root of the sum of all the error variance components). The unbalanced data sets caused by missing observations make it difficult to construct confidence intervals analytically.

Chapter 2
LITERATURE IN VARIANCE COMPONENT ESTIMATIONS, LARGE-SCALE ASSESSMENTS, AND MISSING DATA

Despite the efforts made in measurement research to deal with the limitations encountered when analyzing unbalanced data via G theory, the research in this area suffers from major restrictions. In this chapter, I introduce the applications of G theory in norm-referenced and criterion-referenced testing. Next, I review the advantages and disadvantages of a variety of methods for handling large and unbalanced data sets. Last, I summarize studies that provide a foundation for the proposed subdividing method.

2.1 INDICES COMMONLY USED IN CRITERION REFERENCED AND NORM-REFERENCED TESTS

None of the research conducted for missing data in G theory has investigated the behavior of composite indices that are used for rank ordering examinees and compared the performance of examinees to a criterion. Brennan (1992) and Satterthwaite (1941 & 1946) have provided computational formulas for confidence intervals and standard errors for the various composite indices. Unfortunately, those formulas were derived for balanced data. Given the importance of the composite indices, additional research is needed to examine the confidence intervals and standard error of measurement for those indices. The applications and importance of those composite indices are discussed in the following sections. Appendix A shows the equations for the composite indices.

2.1.1. Reliability Coefficients

The generalizability coefficient (denoted $E\rho^2$) and the dependability coefficient (denoted ϕ) are important in many aspects. Much like the classical test reliability coefficient, the generalizability coefficient has various advantageous for making educational decisions. The coefficient $E\rho^2$ can be defined as the square correlation of test scores between two randomly parallel test forms (Crocker & Algina, 1986, p. 124) assembled in the same universe of generalization (Brennan, 1992, p.3; Cronbach et al., 1972, pp. 18-23; Shavelson & Webb, 1991, pp.12-13). Put differently, the generalizability coefficient shows how well one can rank order students in the same manner using two test forms (or two similar measurement procedures from the same universe of generalization), which were assembled in accordance with the conditions to which one would want to infer. Understanding how well randomly parallel forms rank order test scores is useful in both classroom assessments and large-scale assessments. Frequently, testing agencies or classroom teachers need to prepare several tests containing different samples of questions drawn from the same domain of knowledge. In order to compare students or to evaluate instructions based on test scores obtained from the two randomly parallel forms, one has to estimate the generalizability coefficient. A high generalizability coefficient warrants the comparisons of student learning and teaching practice, because we know that a large portion of the test score variation is due to the variation in students' ability rather than the discrepancies in difficulty of two forms.

Another advantage of the generalizability coefficient is that its transformation ($\sqrt{\rho^2}$) can be used to indicate the degree to which observed scores correlate with universe scores. The higher $\sqrt{\rho^2}$, the more confident one can be when using students' test scores to infer to how much they would know if the students were tested on a broader scope (e.g., test students on all the items in the item bank). Another reason that reliability coefficients are important is that they can be used for criterion-referenced decisions. The dependability coefficient is an index monitoring the degree to which a test can be used to make absolute decisions (e.g., Can an examinee master half of the test items in the domain? How reliably could a measurement procedure determine that a random examinee passes a criterion?). Also, the dependability coefficient can be used to approximate other indices. One such index is the criterion-referenced reliability coefficient denoted $\phi(\lambda)$ (Brennan & Kane, 1977). This index is derived to summarize the relationship between cut-scores and the consistency of a measurement procedure. Patterson (1985, p.35) demonstrated that the ϕ is a lower limit of $\phi(\lambda)$. Like the generalizability coefficient, the higher the dependability coefficient, the more reliably one can make an absolute decision.

The dependability coefficient has become more useful as state departments and schools emphasize standards. For instance, Tucker (1998) advocates that education agencies become active in setting and evaluating standards. Dependability coefficients are well suited for this purpose because one can use dependability coefficients to forecast the consistency of a measurement procedure in relation to where one sets the standard.

Regardless of the wide range of possible applications of reliability coefficients, one cannot take full advantage of those coefficients unless they are estimated accurately. Reliability coefficients, like many other statistics, are subject to sampling errors. Two statistical properties are important for the interpretation of estimates of reliability coefficients in G theory (Personal communication from Gordon, 1998; Vickers, 1998; & Welch, 1996): unbiasedness and efficiency. (See Aczel, 1996; and Hays & Winkler,1970). The current monograph summarizes two data-collection procedures frequently appearing in the literature, and examines these properties of the variance components estimated by the subdividing method.

2.1.2. Standard Error of Measurement (SEM)

The SEMs based on relative and absolute decisions are effective for evaluating the improvement of measurement procedures (Brennan, Gao, and Colton, 1995). As pointed out by many researchers, measurement procedures can be made more reliable in three ways. Kane (1982) provided a succinct account, noting that one could improve the quality of a measurement procedure by taking any or all of the following three actions: 1) restricting the universe of generalization; 2) increasing the measurement conditions in a measurement procedure such as using more items and more raters; and 3) standardizing measurement procedures. Brennan, Gao and Colton (1995) advocated the use of SEMs, in place of the generalizability coefficient, to monitor the improvement of measurement procedures because SEMs are more sensitive to change in error variances than is the generalizability coefficient. This occurs because the universe score variance is larger than error variances and so reduction in error variances is not well reflected in the generalizability coefficient. To use the SEM as an index of quality improvement, one would compare the ratio (the SEM divided by the total variation) obtained before and after the improvement of a measurement procedure.

Besides the monitoring feature just mentioned, Brennan, Gao, and Colton (1995) demonstrated a wide variety of applications based on the SEMs. First, one can use the SEMs to construct confidence intervals for students' universe scores (true scores based on repeated testing). For instance, with the use of the absolute SEM, Brennan, Gao, and Colton (1995) showed that a 95% confidence interval for the mean on a writing test based on a 0 to 5 scale would cover a range of 1.5 points. The writing test had six prompts and each prompt was judged by two raters.

Another application that Brennan, Gao, and Colton (1995) described was to use the SEM to examine the probability that an examinee's true score is within a certain range of his or her observed score. One can ask "What is the probability that a student's true score lies between 3 and 5 given that he or she scored a 4 on the test?" Despite the ease of interpretation of this index, Cronbach, Linn, Brennan, & Haertel (1997) suggested researchers examine the distributional properties of this index before applying it to high stakes decisions. However, examining the SEM in unbalanced situations is not a trivial issue. To this end, I examine the properties of this index for unbalanced designs.

2.1.3. Misclassification Rate for Conjunctive Decision Rules

The generalizability coefficient is particularly important for criterion-referenced examinations such as certification exams (Mehrens, 1987), because it is used to investigate how many additional tasks or raters are needed to reduce the misclassification rate in a D-study. One can ask, "How many added raters or tasks are needed to reduce a misclassification rate to, for example, 0.01, in a writing test?" Cronbach et al. (1997) further elaborated this application to include misclassification rates when using compound decision rules (conjunctive rules). For instance, on a writing test with two writing prompts, one can use the SEM to find out the probability of misclassification of a random student who has received two scores of 2.5 (observed scores) on the two prompts, given that the student deserves two scores of 3.5 (has universe scores of 3.5). In Cronbach et al.'s (1997) example, they showed that one could obtain a probability of incorrectly classifying an examinee in a 6-task assessment. Assuming the hypothetical examinee had universe scores 2.5, 2.5, 2.5, 3.5, 3.5, 3.5, Cronbach et al. (1997) demonstrated that with an absolute SEM of 0.7, the examinee had roughly a 25% chance of having one or more true scores less than 1.5. See Appendix C for the details of the computation of this classification rate.

2.2. ANALYZING MISSING DATA IN G THEORY

Rater errors (e.g., Brennan, 1992a; Saal, Downey, and Lahey, 1980) are not negligible in large-scale assessments (Cronbach, Bradburn, and Horvitz, 1994; Koretz, Stecher, Klein, and McCaffery, 1994; Patz, 1996; Wainer, 1993) as they can affect valid score interpretations (Messick, 1989; Nitko, 1996). Many researchers (e.g. Chiu, 1999; Donoghue and Hombo, 2000; Fleiss, 1981; Hoyt, 2000; Patz, 1996; Wolfe, Chiu, and Myford, 2000) continue to develop techniques in detecting rater errors with a goal to maintain a fair assessment system involving human judgments. Regardless of the popularity of G theory, its applications are limited in large-scale performance assessments due to the unbalanced data caused by test design.

Researchers such as Brennan (1992) have classified unbalanced situations in G theory into two categories, namely unbalanced in terms of nesting and unbalanced in terms of missing data. Methods such as multivariate G theory (Brennan, 1992; Cronbach et al., 1972) have been used to handle unbalancing in terms of nesting, in which the numbers of test questions vary across batteries of a test. Multivariate G theory, however, does not account for missing data in performance assessments. Other methods for handling missing data have limitations that make them inappropriate for large-scale assessments.

The Henderson Methods I and II (Analysis of Variance (ANOVA)-like methods, Henderson, 1953) are incompatible with the conceptual framework in G theory and are computationally extensive (Brennan, Jarjoura, and Deaton, 1980, pp. 37-38). These methods use quadratic forms analogous to the sums of squares of balanced data. The expected values of the quadric forms are then functionally expressed in terms of the variance components. The set of equations characterizing this functional relationship is solved for the variance components. The demerit of these methods is that the quadratic forms are computationally extensive for large amounts of data given that only one unit is observed per cell in the G theory framework (e.g., Brennan, Jarjoura, and Deaton, 1980, p. 37).

Generalizability analyses frequently involve both fixed effects and random effects (Brennan, 1992, pp.76-77). For instance, in performance assessment, one may wish to examine the reliability of using the same raters over time, but using different sets of essay questions in each administration. In this case, the rater facet is fixed whereas the essay facet is considered random. Henderson's Method I, however, is incapable of estimating variance components for such a mixed model (Searle, Casella, and McCulloch, p.189) because it does not restrict the sum of the deviations (from the mean) for the fixed effects to be zero. Without this restriction, the property of unbiased variance component estimates is of questionable value (Brennan, Jarjoura, and Deaton, 1980, p.37). Although Henderson' Method II can handle mixed-effect models, it has limitations, as it cannot be used when there are interactions between fixed and random effects (Searle, Casella, and McCulloch, 1992). In addition, these ANOVA-like methods produced biased estimates in unbalanced situations (Marcoulides, 1988; Olsen, Seely, & Birkes, 1976; Searle, 1971).

Even though Henderson's Method III overcomes the shortcomings of Methods I and II, it produces different estimates for variance components depending upon the order in which the variance components are estimated (Babb, 1986; Brennan, Jarjoura, and Dealton, 1980; and Searle, Casella, and McCulloch, 1992). The choice can be critical since there is usually little justification about which variance components should be estimated first. Without a unique set of estimates for variance components, Henderson's Method III makes the interpretation of generalizability analyses inconclusive. This disadvantage is magnified in computing composite indices (e.g., SEM and reliability coefficients) in generalizability analysis because this method can yield many different composite indices for the same set of data.

Using a two-faceted crossed model, Marcoulides (1988, 1990) randomly deleted observations to compare two estimation methods, ANOVA and Restricted Maximum Likelihood (REML) for data sets with small sample sizes (25 persons, 2 occasions, and 4 raters). He concluded that the REML method was more stable in estimating variance components than the ANOVA method. However, he did not examine the performance of the REML method for large-scale data sets such as those that are common in large-scale performance assessments (e.g., essay writing). As was noted by Babb (1986, p.3), Bell (1985), Rao (1997), and Searle, Casella, and McCulloch (1992), the REML method requires extensive calculations that are infeasible for large data sets. Even for ANOVA methods, the model matrix was frequently very large and thus was too large to invert (Brennan, 1992, p.107; Matherson, 1998).

Cornfield and Tukey (1956), Kirk (1982), Millman (1967), and Searle, Casella, and McCulloch (1992) discuss concise algorithms to determine the coefficients used in the Expected Mean Square (EMS) equations for the estimation of variance components. Those algorithms are so simple that they can be implemented by hand calculations. One needs to know only the numbers of levels in each factor of the ANOVA design. However, one cannot apply the algorithms to unbalanced designs because the numbers of levels in unbalanced designs vary depending upon how many data points exist in each factor. In order to determine the EMS equation, extremely large design matrices had to be created for each factor, including the interaction factors. This is problematic especially for G theory analysis because the object of measurement (Cronbach et al., 1972), say examinees, always has a large number of levels (each person is considered as a level). For a data set of 6000 examinees, to model the object of measurement, or the examinee factor, requires a square matrix of 36,000,000 cells.

Babb (1986) pointed out that in the Maximum Likelihood (ML) and REML methods, one has to calculate the inverse of the variance-covariance matrix associated with the observations at each round of iteration. In addition to the extensive resources required for the ML and REML methods, these inversions of large matrices may not always converge. According to Searle et al. (1992), nonconvergerence in REML indicates that the ANOVA model does not fit the data. Just knowing that the ANOVA model does not fit the data gives very little useful information for data analysis because it is not a surprise that the ANOVA model would not fit a large, sparsely filled data matrix. More information is needed. The subdividing method proposed here overcomes this deficit of the REML by analyzing smaller subsets of data which allows one to examine measurement errors in depth. In case model misfit occurs, one may further examine individual data sets that might have contributed to the misfit.

Other estimation methods such as the Minimum Norm Quadratic Unbiased Estimation (MINQUE) also have problems. In order to assume non-negative estimates for variance components, constraints must be imposed on the parameter space associated with the variance components. Those constraints can cause the quadratic unbiased estimation methods (e.g., MINQUE) to be biased (e.g., Babb, 1986). In a relatively recent publication, Longford (1995) derived two ANOVA models to estimate variance components for essay rating. His models were designed to estimate variance components different than those typically used in the G theory framework. Specifically, the models did not estimate interaction effects. For instance, the *person-by-rater* interaction and *rater-by-item* interaction variance components common in a two-faceted generalizability analysis were not estimated in Longford's model (p. 79 - 82). In addition, the universe-score variance component (variation among examinees, also denoted σ^2_p) was not estimated. With Longford's models, one could not compute the generalizability coefficient for making norm-referenced decisions, which is based on the variance components of interaction effects.

Luecht and Smith (1989) conducted Monte Carlo simulations to examine the extent to which bootstrapping could produce unbiased estimates using a one-facet balanced design with various number of levels in the design. The largest data set simulated was 150 by 150, which did not reflect the amounts of data in large-scale performance assessments. The authors found that the single-factor bootstrapping method produced reasonably unbiased estimates for one-facet *crossed* designs. Nonetheless, they concluded that "the applicability of this technique to more complex designs or nonorthogonal designs, or merely non-normal data, requires further work." (p.20). The conclusion precludes us from applying bootstrapping to complex designs employed in performance assessments (e.g., a *person-by-item-by-rater* design).

2.3. HISTORICAL APPROACHES TO ANALYZING MISSING DATA

Little and Rubin (1987) reviewed historical approaches for handling missing data and proposed various likelihood-based approaches to the analysis of missing data. In their summary (see pp. 40-47 of their book), Little and Rubin (1987) pointed out that these methods did not necessarily produce accurate results and the accuracy depended upon the assumptions to be made about the missing values and the nature (i.e., categorical vs. continuous) of the observed data.

"Complete-case analysis" (Little & Rubin, 1987) is frequently referred to as "listwise deletion" by some researchers and commercial statistical packages. In this method, one analyzes only complete cases, where all variables of interest are present. A critical concern with this method is whether the selection of complete cases leads to biases in sample estimates. This method yields seriously biased results if the complete cases were not a random subsample of the original cases (1987, p.40). Complete-case analysis requires discarding data in a G theory framework to obtain a balanced design. This approach may be employed when a small number of raters make up a pool of raters from which pairs of raters are randomly assigned to score an examinee's response. In such a case, each pair of raters scores a small number of examinees in common. The pair of raters with the largest number of examinees in common may be chosen as the target of the analyses in such a setting, and the scores assigned by the remaining raters are ignored. Unfortunately, by ignoring large portions of the data, this approach jeopardizes the external validity of the study (i.e., the chosen pair of raters may not be representative of the universe of raters).

The "available-case methods" (Little & Rubin, 1987, pp.41-43) are another quick but unsatisfactory alternative for handling multiple outcomes with missing values. One such method, also known as pairwise deletion by some data analysts, estimates covariation for two variables based on cases for which responses to both variables are present. Pairwise deletion can be implemented in the context of Generalizability theory. Such approach that may be employed in an attempt to rectify the shortcoming of the listwise deletion to some extent is to perform analyses on ALL fully-crossed subsets of data within a large data set, making comparisons across these data sets. Although this approach is considerably more desirable than the complete-case method, it still fails to take full advantage of all of the information contained in the entire data set.

Little and Rubin (1987) indicated that a criticism of pairwise deletion is that it can yield correlation estimates that lie outside the range (-1,1), unlike the possible range of a population correlation. This can happen if the sample covariance and the sample variances are based on different cases. (See Appendix D for an example.) Little and Rubin (1987, p.43) also pointed out that available-case methods can lead to paradoxical conclusions when missing values are systematic, rather than randomly distributed. In their example, one could find that two variables, say A and B, were each perfectly correlated with a third variable, say C (i.e., $r_{AC} = r_{BC} = 1$), yet these two variables showed absolutely no correlation with one another in the samples of observed values ($r_{AB} = 0$). See Appendix E for a hypothetical example of this situation. One other disadvantage of the available-case methods is that they may produce covariance matrices that are not positive definite, a property required by many analyses based on the covariance matrix, including multiple regression. Kim and Curry (1977) and Little and Rubin (1987, p.43) concluded that if the data were Missing Completely at Random (MCAR) and correlations were modest, the available-case methods were more desirable than the complete-case analysis, because they did not waste as many data points as the complete-case analysis did.

The current study investigated one option for analyzing missing data that preserves both the internal and external validity of the Generalizability Study (G study, Brennan, 1992a) while more fully utilizing the information contained in the data set. According to the literature, such a method for subdividing a large data set into mutually-exclusive and exhaustive subsets for the purpose of creating multiple data sets that are fully-analyzable in a generalizability theory framework has not been proposed. The goal of this method is to obtain the most accurate G study variance component estimates possible so that generalizations beyond that data set will be valid.

2.4. IMPUTATION AS A METHOD TO HANDLE MISSING DATA

In addition to the aforementioned historical approaches, Little and Rubin (1987, pp.39-71) summarized major imputation methods (methods to fill in sparsely filled data) that are commonly used in sample surveys. These methods, however, were not always applicable to analyses of assessments, tests, or examinations usually designed to measure fewer constructs (which are manifested as groups of test items) than sample surveys are designed to measure. Imputation methods often replace missing values by other observed values in the same survey. Assessments, particularly performance based assessments, do not always have as many items as in sample surveys or in national tests. Performance-based tasks such as writing prompts are frequently scored as separate items. Because of cost and time constraints, very few items are typically administered in performance assessments. In fact, in all the examples of large-scale examinations that follow, very few items were administered. Frequently, large-scale tests administer only two items (The Collegiate Assessment of Academic Proficiency, Authors, 1998). Some tests administer even just one item (The 1998 NAEP Writing Assessment, U.S. Department of Education, 1998; The TOEFL Test of Written English test, Authors, 1998b). Putting aside other controversial reservations against imputation, having too few items makes imputation impractical for performance assessments.

2.5. POTENTIAL SOLUTIONS IN HANDLING MISSING DATA IN G THEORY

Smith (1978) examined the variability (stability) of the variance components for a two-facet crossed model. This model is a major model used in performance assessment (e.g., the person-by-tasks-by-rater design). With a focus on the variance component of the person effect, Smith (1978) found that the stability of variance component estimates varied. Variability depended on several factors, including the number of levels in the facets and the complexity of the expected mean square equations used for estimation. Smith found that operational data sets always were very large, and frequently, large data sets contain unbalanced designs, which can cause unstable variance component estimates. He also found that changing the configuration (e.g., from a crossed model to a *nested* model) affected the stability of variance components like that for the person effect. Therefore, Smith (1981) suggested the use of multiple generalizability analyses {e.g., P:(SxI:F) and I:(FxP:S) }}[1] in place of a large and complex model (e.g, P:SxI:F) because the expected mean square equations are less complicated and so one would obtain more stable variance component estimates. Smith (1978; 1981) called for further examinations of the use of multiple generalizability analyses in the context of unbalanced situations. Unfortunately, according to the Social Science Citation Index (1978 - present), no follow-up research has been conducted to examine the generalization of the Smith method.

Unsatisfied with the limitations of the MIVQUE, MINQUE, ML, and REML methods, Babb (1986) developed a model and notation for pooling estimates of variance components obtained from subsets of unbalanced data. According to Babb (1986), one can partition data into subsets, each small enough to allow ML and REML estimation to be computationally feasible. Then, one can pool variance component estimates obtained from subsets of unbalanced data. Though the Babb models and notations were invented for unbalanced designs, one can adopt his approach to handle balanced data because balanced data can be construed as a special case of unbalanced data (Searle, Casella, & McCulloch, 1992). However, due to insufficient time, computation resources, and financial support, Babb (1986) did not demonstrate the extent to which the pooled method worked for unbalanced data. Babb (1986) and Searle, Casella, and McCulloch (1992) called for further research. In particular, they suggested one use Monte Carlo simulation to validate the pooled method (e.g., Babb, 1986, p.26). Regardless of the potential usefulness of Babb's approach, no other studies have followed up with that research. (No research has referenced Babb in the Social Science Citation Index from 1981 to present).

Independent of Babb (1986) and Smith (1978, 1981), Chiu and Wolfe (1997) applied a subdividing method to analyze unbalanced performance assessment data and concluded that the subdividing method was practical and provided stable results in estimating variance components. Chiu and Wolfe's (1997) subdividing method differed from those of Babb (1986) and Smith (1978, 1981) in the following ways. Smith (1981) advocated using multiple generalizability analyses to reduce complexities in design configurations (e.g.,

---

[1] P:(SxI):F is the shorthand notation for a three faceted design in which different test forms (F) contain different sets of items (I). The testing agent administered any one of the forms to every school (S). Students (P) in a school responded to only a portion of the items administered to the school.

use the P:(SxI:F) and I:(FxP:S) designs to estimate variance components in the P:SxI:F design). Chiu and Wolfe (1997) proposed to divide a large data set into many smaller data sets with similar configuration (i.e., divide a large two-facet data set into multiple smaller two-facet data sets). Despite the distinctions, both Chiu and Wolfe (1997) and Smith (1981) had the same purpose, which was to obtain more stable estimates for the variance components. Babb (1986) developed notation and models to combine variance components from balanced and unbalanced data subsets. For balanced data, Babb (1986, p.22) showed that one pooled estimator of a variance component was the simple arithmetic average of the estimators obtained for each individual data subset. For unbalanced data, he used an approximation to estimate the covariances of variance components. Those covariances were then used in estimating the pooled variance components. Babb (1986), however, did not examine how to combine variance components for the *modified balanced incomplete block* design frequently used in essay reading. (In this design, examinees respond to two essays and each essay is graded by two raters, one rater grades both essays and is paired with a different rater on each essay). Although Chiu and Wolfe (1997) combined variance components for *crossed*, *nested*, and *MBIB* designs, they applied their method to only a single data set. They did not examine the performance of that method in other data sets.

Three other studies also employed methods similar to the proposed subdividing method. Lane, Liu, Ankenmann, and Stone (1996) examined the generalizability and validity of a mathematics performance assessment using a two facet design, the *person* x *rater* x *task* design (denoted p x r x t). Due to large and unbalanced data, they divided their data sets into 17 smaller subsets of *crossed* design (p.81). Brennan, Gao, and Colton (1995) employed three completely *crossed* designs to examine the generalizability of a listening and a writing test. They then suggested that one might consider pooling the results from the three crossed data subsets to judge the reliability of those two measurement procedures. Linn, Burton, DeStefano, and Hanson (1996) conducted a pilot study to examine the generalizability of a mathematics test and used six two-faceted crossed designs (p x r x t). Unlike the Chiu and Wolfe (1997) study, in which they dev eloped and examined the subdividing method, all three aforementioned studies focused on the interpretations of the results based on the unverified subdividing method. None of the four studies investigated the performance and generalization of the subdividing method.

2.6. SUMMARY OF LITERATURE REVIEW

This chapter reviewed the advantages and disadvantages of a number of methods (i.e., imputation, listwise and pairwise deletions, ANOVA methods, MINQUE, ML, and REML) and concluded that all of these methods were disadvantageous in analyzing large amounts of unbalanced data. They were either unable to produce unbiased variance component estimates or required excessive computational power for obtaining G theory estimates. In addition, none of these methods investigated the relationship between the accuracy and precision of the estimates and the pattern and amounts of missing data in the context of performance assessments. Engelhard (1997) surveyed various ways of constructing rater and task banks and showed how missing data were manifested in these rater and task banks. However, Engelhard (1997) focused on exemplifying different rater and task banks rather than investigating how rater and task banks influenced the estimation of measurement errors in the G theory framework. Searle (1987) suggested one use "subset analysis" to analyze unbalanced data using ANOVA models. This method, however, was not examined in the context of G theory. In addition, Searle (1987) did not relate the accuracy and precision of variance component estimates to the pattern and amounts of unbalanced data. Babb (1985) was the closest study to the current monograph as Babb described how to modify the General Linear Model to analyze subsets of data. Nonetheless, he did not verify his method because of the lack of computational resources to conduct a simulation study.

The current research study investigates a subdividing method, which allows investigators to utilize unbalanced data to estimate variance components while requiring low computational power. The current study also sets out to examine the extent to which the decision rules used to set up a scoring procedure influence the accuracy and precision of G theory estimates. The decision rules used to set up a scoring procedure are coined "rating plans" and they are studied with other factors to determine in what circumstances the subdividing method can perform optimally. Specifically, the current study examines these factors: *rating plans, variations in item difficulty* and in *rater inconsistency, number of examinees, number of raters,* and *number of tasks scored by a common group of raters*. Chapter 3 reveals the rationales for choosing these factors.

Chapter 3
METHODOLOGY

This chapter first summarizes the procedures of the subdividing method, then lists research questions tailored to the rating of student work in performance assessments. Next, it describes the conditions to vary, the data generation procedures, and then the outcomes used to evaluate the subdividing method. The design of a Monte Carlo simulation study (Mooney, 1997; Rubinstein, 1981) is discussed in detail in the context of "rating plans", which are sets of rules used to assign examinees and tasks to raters during scoring sessions.

Monte Carlo studies (Cronbach et al., 1972; Mooney, 1997) are especially suitable for the current study because one can evaluate the practicality and statistical properties (e.g., bias and efficiency) of an estimation method by comparing the estimated parameters to the known population parameters. In the measurement context, it is infeasible to conduct many reliability experiments in which actual raters and examinees are crossed. Also, it is difficult to imagine how one could control precisely raters' severity, leniency, and inconsistency for such experiments. In addition, the real problem is that one cannot evaluate estimation methods based on data for which one does not know the population parameters. These restrictions make Monte Carlo studies especially appropriate for examining this subdividing method. Furthermore, as has been pointed out by many researchers (e.g., Harwell, Stone, Hsu, & Kirisci, 1996; Longford, 1995; Psychometrika Editorial Board, 1979), analytical methods (e.g., deriving expected mean squares equations) can be inadequate for the examination of statistical properties in generalizability analysis (especially for composite indices). Unlike analytical methods, simulation studies can be used even if probabilities of selection (determined by the amount of missing data), sample sizes, and the magnitude of variance components are treated as independent variables. Also, Monte Carlo methods are especially suitable when it is difficult to satisfy asymptotic assumptions because only a small number of levels are sampled in each factors (e.g., only two levels in the item facets, $n_i = 2$).

3.1. PROCEDURES OF THE SUBDIVING METHOD

The subdividing method has three stages. They are the 1) Modeling, 2) Estimating, and 3) Synthesizing stages. The sections that follow illustrate each of these stages in detail.

3.1.1. Modeling Stage

In the first step, the sparsely filled data set is divided into smaller subsets of balanced data that exhibit structural designs common in Analysis of Variance, namely the *crossed* design, the *nested* design, and the *modified balanced incomplete block design* (*MBIB*). The sparsely-filled data set is divided into S_t data subsets, with t = 1, 2, or 3, and with S_t indicating the number of subsets in each of the *crossed* (S_1), *nested* (S_2), and *MBIB* (S_3) designs, respectively. Note that the *crossed* and *nested* designs are structural designs that are common in generalizability analysis. A *MBIB* design is formed every time one rater scores both items and is paired with a different second rater on each item. See Appendix F for the structure of the *MBIB* design. Chiu and Wolfe (1997) provide a detailed description of the algorithm used to divide an unbalanced data into subsets of data. In the paragraphs that follow, I first illustrate the algorithm followed by developing the notation that can be used to implement the algorithm.

Steps for the Modeling Stage

This section illustrates how to restructure a hypothetical sparsely-filled data matrix into smaller subsets for generalizability analyses. The goal is to show how nearly all of the information can be considered without resorting to "discarding" data or ignoring distinctions by "collapsing" across elements (e.g., individual raters) of the measurement design. The G study results from the various designs that I describe can be averaged to produce a single set of variance components for the entire data set. In the following examples, I describe a measurement context in which fifteen examinees each answers two test items which are rated by any two of four raters (named A, B, C, and D). That is, the design of our G study contains two facets: (a) items and (b) raters and can be represented as a fully-crossed examinee × item × rater (15 × 2 × 4) design with many missing observations. Figure 1 depicts such a data matrix. This matrix indicates which two raters rated a particular examinee on the two items. For instance, the four scores in the first row show that Examinee 1 was rated by Rater A and Rater B on both of the items.

	Item 1				Item 2			
Examinees	Rater A	Rater B	Rater C	Rater D	Rater A	Rater B	Rater C	Rater D
1	$X_{1,1,A}$	$X_{1,1,B}$			$X_{1,2,A}$	$X_{1,2,B}$		
2			$X_{2,1,C}$	$X_{2,1,D}$			$X_{2,2,C}$	$X_{2,2,D}$
3	$X_{3,1,A}$	$X_{3,1,B}$			$X_{3,2,A}$	$X_{3,2,B}$		
4			$X_{4,1,C}$	$X_{4,1,D}$			$X_{4,2,C}$	$X_{4,2,D}$
5	$X_{5,1,A}$	$X_{5,1,B}$					$X_{5,2,C}$	$X_{5,2,D}$
6	$X_{6,1,A}$	$X_{6,1,B}$					$X_{6,2,C}$	$X_{6,2,D}$
7		$X_{7,1,B}$	$X_{7,1,C}$		$X_{7,2,A}$			$X_{7,2,D}$
8	$X_{8,1,A}$		$X_{8,1,C}$			$X_{8,2,B}$		$X_{8,2,D}$
9	$X_{9,1,A}$		$X_{9,1,C}$			$X_{9,2,B}$		$X_{9,2,D}$
10		$X_{10,1,B}$	$X_{10,1,C}$		$X_{10,2,A}$			$X_{10,2,D}$
11	$X_{11,1,A}$	$X_{11,1,B}$			$X_{11,2,A}$		$X_{11,2,C}$	
12	$X_{12,1,A}$	$X_{12,1,B}$				$X_{12,2,B}$	$X_{12,2,C}$	
13	$X_{13,1,A}$		$X_{13,1,C}$			$X_{13,2,B}$	$X_{13,2,C}$	
14	$X_{14,1,A}$	$X_{14,1,B}$			$X_{14,2,A}$	$X_{14,2,B}$		
15		$X_{15,1,B}$	$X_{15,1,C}$		$X_{15,2,A}$			$X_{15,2,D}$

Note: Rows represent examinees, columns represent items, and sub-columns represent raters. This matrix contains scores assigned by two raters (selected from the pool of four) to each examinee's response to each item. Subscripts represent examinees, items, and raters.

Figure 1: A hypothetical data matrix.

We can use three methods to decompose the entire data set into exhaustive subsets. That is, the sum of the number of observations analyzed by these three methods will equal the number of observations in the original data set. The data matrices from these subsets of data can each be analyzed under a unique G study design. For the first method, the crossed method, we extract all possible fully-crossed subsets of the data from the original data set so that each subset of data contains all examinees who were rated by a specific pair of raters on both items.

For example, Rater A and Rater B rated the response to both the first and the second item (i.e., AB, AB; where Item 1 and Item 2 are separated by a comma) for Examinees 1, 3, and 14. In this crossed design, each data set contains only scores assigned by a single pair of raters. Figure 2 shows how the information in Figure 1 decomposes into several crossed data sets. Responses of Examinees 1, 3, and 14 are rated by the same two raters (A and B) on both items, and for this reason scores for these two examinees are extracted from the entire data set and are stored in a smaller subset [i.e., Crossed(1)] containing scores given by only this pair of raters. In the same figure, Examinees 2 and 4 are graded by both Rater C and Rater D on the two items (CD, CD), and so these cases are extracted and saved in a data set with the label Crossed (2). The "2" in parentheses indicates the data set is a second of the crossed design type. In general, the parenthetical numbers distinguish one data set from the others within a type of design. By going down the rows in the original data matrix, we exhaust all crossed designs and store them in these two subsets.

Examinee	Item 1				Item 2					
	Rater A	Rater B	Rater C	Rater D	Rater A	Rater B	Rater C	Rater D	Data Set	Design (File ID)
1	$X_{1,1,A}$	$X_{1,1,B}$			$X_{1,2,A}$	$X_{1,2,B}$			(AB, AB)	Crossed (1)
2			$X_{2,1,C}$	$X_{2,1,D}$			$X_{2,2,C}$	$X_{2,2,D}$	(CD, CD)	Crossed (2)
3	$X_{3,1,A}$	$X_{3,1,B}$			$X_{3,2,A}$	$X_{3,2,B}$			(AB, AB)	Crossed (1)
4			$X_{4,1,C}$	$X_{4,1,D}$			$X_{4,2,C}$	$X_{4,2,D}$	(CD, CD)	Crossed (2)
5	$X_{5,1,A}$	$X_{5,1,B}$					$X_{5,2,C}$	$X_{5,2,D}$	(AB, CD)	Nested (1)
6	$X_{6,1,A}$	$X_{6,1,B}$					$X_{6,2,C}$	$X_{6,2,D}$	(AB, CD)	Nested (1)
7		$X_{7,1,B}$	$X_{7,1,C}$		$X_{7,2,A}$			$X_{7,2,D}$	(BC, AD)	Nested (2)
8	$X_{8,1,A}$		$X_{8,1,C}$			$X_{8,2,B}$		$X_{8,2,D}$	(AC, BD)	Nested (3)
9	$X_{9,1,A}$		$X_{9,1,C}$			$X_{9,2,B}$		$X_{9,2,D}$	(AC, BD)	Nested (3)
10		$X_{10,1,B}$	$X_{10,1,C}$		$X_{10,2,A}$			$X_{10,2,D}$	(BC, AD)	Nested (2)
11	$X_{11,1,A}$	$X_{11,1,B}$			$X_{11,2,A}$		$X_{11,2,C}$		(AB, AC)	MBIB (1)
12	$X_{12,1,A}$	$X_{12,1,B}$				$X_{12,2,B}$	$X_{12,2,C}$		(AB, BC)	MBIB (2)
13	$X_{13,1,A}$		$X_{13,1,C}$			$X_{13,2,B}$	$X_{13,2,C}$		(AC, CB)	MBIB (3)
14	$X_{14,1,A}$	$X_{14,1,B}$			$X_{14,2,A}$	$X_{14,2,B}$			(AB, AB)	Crossed (1)
15		$X_{15,1,B}$	$X_{15,1,C}$		$X_{15,2,A}$			$X_{15,2,D}$	(BC, AD)	Nested (2)

Note: The last two columns illustrate how to restructure the sparse data set into multiple smaller data sets analyzable by the three methods, namely the *crossed*, *MBIB*, and *nested* methods.

Figure 2: The implementation matrix of the data matrix in Figure 1.

A nested design is formed every time one pair of raters rates the first item and a completely different rater pair rates the second item (e.g., Rater A and Rater B rate Item 1 and Rater C and Rater D rate Item 2; denoted AB, CD). Using the same algorithm as for extracting crossed data sets, we extract all nested subsets so that each nested data set contains scores of examinees who are graded by the same four raters. In Figure 2, Examinees 5 and 6 are graded by

Raters A and B on Item 1 and Raters C and D on Item 2 (AB, CD). As a result, these examinees' scores are stored in one data set which is labeled Nested (1). Similarly, the Nested (2) data set contains all examinees scored by Raters B and C on Item 1 and Raters A and D on Item 2 (BC, AD). The Nested (3) data set contains all examinees graded by Raters A and C on Item 1 and Raters B and D on Item 2 (AC, BD). These three nested data sets exhaust all of the cases of nested designs in the original data set. Hence, we have consumed 12 of the 15 cases with the nested and crossed designs.

The third design, the mixed design, accounts for the remaining cases. A mixed design is formed every time one rater rates both items and is paired with a different second rater on each item. For example, for Examinee 11, Rater A rates both items and is paired with Rater B on Item 1 and Rater C on Item 2 (AB, AC). However, there is a problem with this design -- Rater B and Rater C always rate only one item each so that no information is available for evaluating the item effect for Rater B or Rater C. This problem is resolved by adding into the same data set two other rater combinations, (BA, BC) and (CA,CB). In these two designs Rater B and Rater C rate examinees' responses on both items. As a result, a fully mixed data set contains all mixed examples for a particular triplet of raters. Figure 2 depicts how to identify these three sets of raters and how to extract them from a data set. Because Examinees 11, 12, and 13 are, in turn, double-graded by Raters A, B, and C, the scores of these three examinees are stored in a single data set [Mixed(1)]. Other mixed data sets could be created with the Rater A, B, D; Rater A, C, D; and Rater B, C, D triplets.

Thus, we have been able to recover all the data within the original data set by parsing it into several subsets. Each of these subsets, if analyzed separately, will produce a set of variance component estimates. But, the variance component estimates produced by any one of these separate analyses may not adequately represent the variance structure of the entire data set. Unfortunately, the entire data set usually cannot be adequately analyzed because of weaknesses in the technology (i.e., computational time) or software (i.e., failure to handle missing data) used to perform generalizability analyses. However, we can average the variance components from several G studies (Brennan, Gao, & Colton, 1995) to get more accurate and comprehensive variance component estimates. Hence, we can use our exhaustive parsing method (as described above) to extract all cases from a data set, perform G studies on each of these subsets of the data, and average the variance components across these G studies. These averaged variance components can serve as the information upon which D studies are based. In doing so, we preserve all of the information from the larger data set and create data sets with a structure that can be handled by currently-available computer programs with a minimal processing load.

Notations for the Modeling Stage

I use $n_{f,t,s}$ to represent the numbers of levels in the fth factor, t^{th} design, and s^{th} data subset, where f = {p, i, r, pi, pr, ir, pir} = {1,2,3,4,5,6,7}, t = {*crossed*, *nested*, and *MBIB*} = {1,2,3}, and s = {subset$_1$, subset$_1$, subset S_t} = {1,2, ... S_t}. The unbalanced data set has a sample size of $n_{p\cdot\cdot}$. The number of raters involved to score examinees in the unbalanced data set was denoted $n_{r\cdot\cdot}$ and the number of items administered was denoted $n_{i\cdot\cdot}$. The two periods in the subscript indicate that the sample size was added across different types of design and different data subsets in each design.

With the notation developed above, one can use the General Linear Model (GLM) to structure the data in each subset and then estimate the variance components from those subsets (stage 2), followed by pooling the estimates to obtain an overall estimate for the variance components. The GLM, described in many places, such as Searle et al. (1992), is summarized below. The pooling method is summarized in the subsequent section entitled "Synthesizing Stage". The general linear model is:

$$\vec{y}_s = X_s\beta_s + \sum_{f=1}^{7} Z_{f,s}\mu_{f,s}. \tag{1}$$

The $\vec{y}_s$ in the above equation represents a vector of scores in the sth data subset for each design type. The scores are expressed as a sum of the overall mean and the effects of the seven factors. The grand mean is represented in β_s, a vector of ones. The vector u comprises the means of a single level of each of the seven factors and the design matrices Z contained only zeros and ones to indicate the level to which a score belonged. Utilizing this GLM model, one can disentangle the variations of test scores into multiple facets of variations (Brennan, 1992). The "Estimating Stage" in section 3.1.2 serves this purpose. The following paragraphs illustrate what constitute data subsets and how to determine the number of data subsets can be extracted from a sparsely-filled data set.

Data Subsets

In unbalanced situations, rather than having all raters score all the examinees, sets of raters may score groups of examinees. Sets of raters can be either mutually exclusive or inclusive and this is determined by the rules governing the scoring procedures, termed the "rating plan" in this monograph (this is discussed in detail in subsequent sections). The scores that a collection of raters assigns to a group of students form the basis for conducting a generalizability analysis and so, a collection of raters with a group of students can be construed as a subset of data. Inclusive rater groups share raters and for this reason the number of rater groups always exceeds the number of raters. In a hypothetical scenario with four raters, one could form six rater groups of two raters. Using the letters A, B, C, and D to represent the four hypothetical raters, one could form up to six collections. These six collections are denoted by six pairs of letters as: $\{AB, AC, AD, BC, BD, CD\}$. Since, for example, rater A sat on three rater groups (i.e., $\{AB, AC, AD\}$), these groups were inclusive or connected by rater A.

In another scenario assuming *no connections*, the same four raters would form only two collections of raters, which could be set up in one of the following three ways: $\{AB, CD\}$, $\{AC, BD\}$, or $\{AD, BC\}$. The number of rater groups expands as the number of raters (denoted *size of rater pool* hereafter) increases. If a rater pool was composed of 28 raters, as many as 378 inclusive (*connected*) rater groups could serve to score examinees. Alternatively, these 28 raters would form 14 exclusive (*disconnected*) rater groups. The general equations for determining the number of *connected* and *disconnected* rater groups given that each examinee is responding to one item are:

$$\text{number of connected rater groups (data subsets)} = \binom{n_{r\bullet\bullet}}{2}\text{; and} \tag{2}$$

$$\text{number of disconnected rater groups (data subsets)} = \frac{n_{r\bullet\bullet}}{2}. \tag{3}$$

Assuming that the rater groups score the same number of examinees, then the two types of rater groups would score $n_{p\bullet\bullet} / \binom{n_{r\bullet\bullet}}{2}$ and $n_{p\bullet\bullet} / \frac{n_{r\bullet\bullet}}{2}$ examinees, respectively. In other words, $\binom{n_{r\bullet\bullet}}{2}$ subsets of data each include

$n_{p\bullet\bullet} / \binom{n_{r\bullet\bullet}}{2}$ examinees for a rating plan utilizing *connected* groups, and $\frac{n_{r\bullet\bullet}}{2}$ subsets contain $n_{p\bullet\bullet} / \frac{n_{r\bullet\bullet}}{2}$ examinees for a rating plan utilizing *disconnected* rater groups. The scores that these groups assign to examinees exhibit a crossed structural design when examinees respond to two items and both raters in the same group score both items. The aforementioned GLM model estimates the measurement errors (i.e., variance components) associated with the collections of raters.

The subsequent section entitled "Decision rule for weighting" on page 31 shows a set of general equations, Equations (9), (10), and (11), to predict number of rater groups (data subsets) given the size of rater pool and the *connected* rating plan. That set of general equations was developed for a more flexible *connected* rating plan in which each set of raters was not required to score all items responded to by the examinees.

3.1.2. Estimating Stage

In this stage, variance components are estimated for each subset of data. The ANOVA method (e.g., Brennan, 1992, Searle et al., 1992, p. 173) can be used to estimate variance components for the *crossed* and *nested* designs. For the *MBIB* design, the Minimum Norm Quadratic Unbiased Estimate (MINQUE) method can be used to obtain the variance component estimators (Bell, 1985; Giesbrecht, 1983; Goodnight, 1978; Rao, 1997).

For the ANOVA method, variance components are estimated by solving sets of Expected Mean Squares (EMS) equations (Brennan, 1992, p.130) relating the variance components and mean squares. The EMS of each subset of data is expressed in the following matrix formula, where $\vec{\hat{\sigma}}_s^2$ is a vector of estimated variance components. The estimates are

$$\vec{\hat{\sigma}}_s^2 = C_s^{-1} \vec{a}_s^2, \tag{4}$$

where C_s^{-1} is an f x f upper-triangular matrix of coefficients of the variance components estimated based on the GLM model (Equation (1)), f = 1,2, ..., 7 represent the effects in the sth data subset, and $\vec{a}_s^2$ is a vector of mean squares for the effects observed in the data. The following is a representation of Equation (4) expressed in data matrices:

$$\begin{bmatrix} \hat{\sigma}^2_{s,p} \\ \hat{\sigma}^2_{s,i} \\ \hat{\sigma}^2_{s,r} \\ \hat{\sigma}^2_{s,pi} \\ \hat{\sigma}^2_{s,pr} \\ \hat{\sigma}^2_{s,ir} \\ \hat{\sigma}^2_{s,pir} \end{bmatrix} = \begin{bmatrix} n_i n_r & 0 & 0 & n_r & n_i & 0 & 1 \\ 0 & n_p n_r & 0 & n_r & 0 & n_p & 1 \\ 0 & 0 & n_p n_i & 0 & n_i & n_p & 1 \\ 0 & 0 & 0 & n_r & 0 & 0 & 1 \\ 0 & 0 & 0 & 0 & n_i & 0 & 1 \\ 0 & 0 & 0 & 0 & 0 & n_p & 1 \\ 0 & 0 & 0 & 0 & 0 & 0 & 1 \end{bmatrix}^{-1} \begin{bmatrix} MS_{s,p} \\ MS_{s,i} \\ MS_{s,r} \\ MS_{s,pi} \\ MS_{s,pr} \\ MS_{s,ir} \\ MS_{s,pir} \end{bmatrix}.$$

The C_s^{-1} matrix shows the numbers of levels for each factor. The computational formula for C_s^{-1}, derived by Searle et al. (1992, p. 173, Equation 18), is described in Equation (5).

$$C_s^{-1} = \{\ {}_m trace(Z'_{s,j}\ A_{s,j}\ Z_{s,j})\ \}_{i,j}, \tag{5}$$

where $m = m_{ij}$ refers to the ith row and j^{th} column in C_s^{-1}. The Z matrices are the design matrices for each of the effects in the GLM model shown in Equation (1). The A matrices are symmetric matrices obtained in the quadratic forms when computing the sums of squares for each factor.

The sizes of the Z matrices depend on the numbers of levels in the factors (also termed as *facets* in G theory). In the context of G theory, the person facet always has a large number of levels and so the Z matrices can be too large to process, for example when there are 6000 examinees (yielding a square matrix with 36,000,000 entries). The subdividing method overcomes this restriction by dividing the large data set into smaller subsets so that the A matrices for the subsets are small enough to be processed. For instance, a subset of 100 examinees exhibiting a crossed structure has a square matrix $A_{s,j}$ of dimension 100 x 100, with 10,000 entries, which is considerably smaller than the 36,000,000 described above when $n = 6000$.

Assuming a multivariate normal distribution for the score effects, the variance-covariance matrix associated with the estimated variance components in $\bar{\hat{\sigma}}_s^2$ is (Brennan, 1992, p. 133):

$$\hat{V}_{t,s} = C_{t,s}^{-1} D_{t,s} (C_{t,s}^{-1})' \tag{6}$$

where t = {*crossed* or *nested*} and $D_{t,s}$ is an f x f diagonal matrix containing the diagonal elements $2(MS_j)^2/(df_j + 2)$. Note that the index j = 1, 2, ... f designates the score effects in a design including both main effects and interaction effects.

3.1.3. Synthesizing Stage

Meta-analysis (Hedges and Olkin, 1995), a quantitative method to summarize research results, is especially suitable for the subdividing method because it is capable of estimating an overall outcome based on many outcomes obtained from individual empirical studies, or, here, data subsets. Thus, meta-analytic methods were used to aggregate variance components from each subset of data. In the Synthesis Stage, data subsets were weighted by subset sample size and then variance components were pooled. Composite indices were computed on the basis of those pooled variance component estimates.

Weighted estimates of the variance components can be obtained by weighting the data subsets by their sample sizes across all subsets from both the *disconnected crossed* and *connected mixture* rating plans. For factor f we obtain

$$\hat{\sigma}_f^2 = \overline{\sigma}_f^2 = \frac{\sum_{t=1}^{T}\sum_{s=1}^{S_t} n_{p,t,s}\,\hat{\sigma}_{f,s}^2}{\sum_{t=1}^{T}\sum_{s=1}^{S_t} n_{p,t,s}}, \tag{7}$$

where $f = \begin{cases} p, i, r, pi, pr, ir, \text{ and } pir & \text{for a } crossed \text{ or } MBIB \text{ design} \\ p, i, r{:}i, pi, \text{ and } p{:}ri & \text{for a } nested \text{ design} \end{cases}$

s = the sth data subset

t = the tth structural design, and

$n_{p,t,s}$ = number of examinees in the sth data subset of the tth structural design.

When the data subsets were equal in sample size (i.e., had the same number of examinees), the weighted average variance component became:

$$\hat{\sigma}_f^2 = \overline{\sigma}_f^2 = \frac{\sum_{s=1}^{S} \hat{\sigma}_{f,s}^2}{S_\bullet}, \qquad (8)$$

where $S_\bullet$ is the number of data subsets across all the structual designs.

The critical questions about weighting are: (a) What are the consequences if weighting is not used when it is needed? and (b) Under which rating plans can weighting be ignored? The simulation study reported below in the Results section addresses question (a). Equation (8) indicates one answer to question (b), which is that weighting is not needed when sample sizes are equal in the data subsets. This occurs when raters evenly share the workload. The answer to question (b) becomes elusive when there is no plan to ensure that raters evenly share the workload. In that case, one has to decide whether or not data subsets are equal in size. The following section provides a decision rule and its validity was tested in the simulation study reported in the Results section.

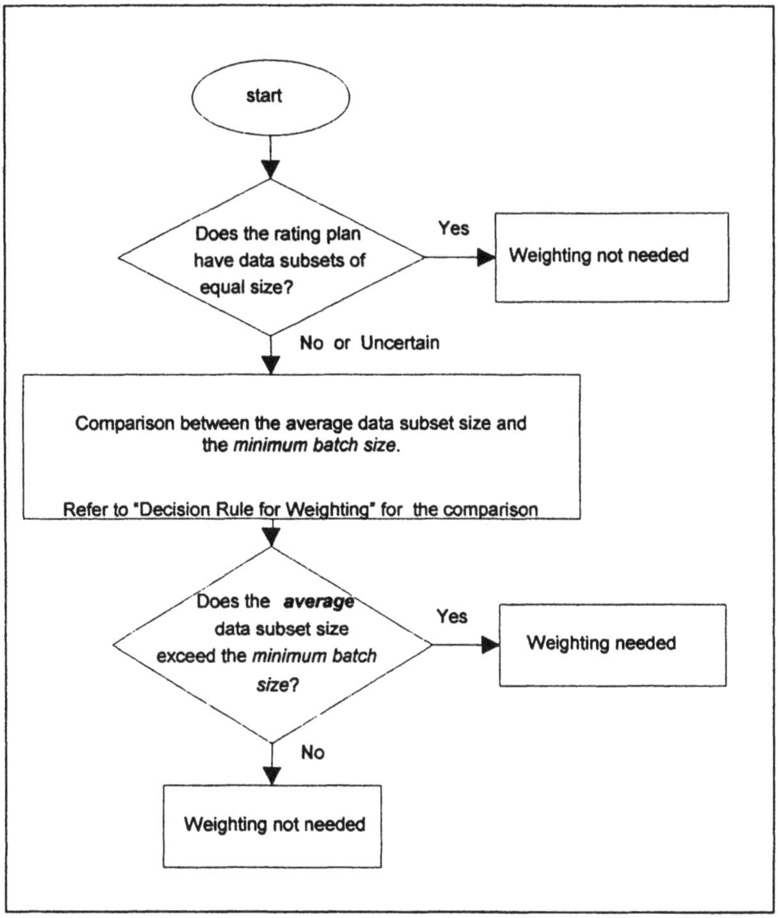

Figure 3: Decision rule for weighting

3.2. DECISION RULE FOR WEIGHTING

If a sparsely filled data set is divided into many subsets containing different numbers of examinees (i.e., sample size), these subsets will have to be weighted in order to provide precise variance component estimates. Data subsets differ in sample as a result of the random process used to assign a large volume of examinees and tasks to a relatively small number of raters. When batches of the work submitted by examinees outnumber the rater groups, some rater groups will have to score more batches than the other groups and thus weighting is needed to account for such a difference. The following are the steps to determine whether or not the number of batches exceeds the number of rater groups.

(I) Compute the total number of possible data subsets, which is the count of all possible data subsets in the structural designs available in the rating plan. For instance, the *connected mixture* rating plan has data sets from three structural designs, where counts are shown here.

The number of *crossed* data subsets, $S_{crossed} = \binom{n_r}{n_{r*}}$, (9)

The number of *MBIB* data subsets, $S_{MBIB} = \binom{n_r}{n_{r*}} n_{r*}(n_r - n_{r*})$, (10)

The number of *nested* data subsets, $S_{nested} = \binom{n_r}{n_{r*}}\binom{n_r - 2}{n_{r*}}$, and (11)

Total number of possible data subsets,

$$S_{\bullet} = S_{crossed} + S_{MBIB} + S_{nested}, \tag{12}$$

where n_{r*} is the number of raters to be subsampled from a pool of n_r raters. It is equivalent to the number of ratings on an item for a given examinee.

(II) Determine whether or not the number of batches $(\frac{n_{p..}}{MinBat})$ exceeds the number of rater groups or potential data subsets ($S_{\bullet}$). If so, then weighting is needed. Alternatively, this decision rule can be expressed in terms of any other forms including the volume of examinees ($n_{p..}$), number of rater groups ($S_{\bullet}$), and minimum batch size (*MinBat*). For example, these three terms can be expressed as follows (if the the following inequality is true for any given sparsely-filled data set, then weighting is needed).

$$n_{p\bullet\bullet} > S_{\bullet} * MinBat \tag{13}$$

For example, given a pool of four raters to score 1500 examinees using a *minimum batch size* of 12, should one weight the data subsets by sample size? The computations and decision for steps I and II are shown below.

(I) Number of *crossed* data subsets, $S_{crossed} = \binom{4}{2} = 6$

Number of *MBIB* data subsets, $S_{MBIB} = \binom{4}{2} 2(4-2) = 24$

Number of *nested* data subsets, $S_{nested} = \binom{4}{2}\binom{4-2}{2} = 6$

Total number of possible data subsets, $S_{\bullet} = 6 + 24 + 6 = 36$

(II) Since there were more batches (i.e., 1500/12 = 125) than possible rater groups (i.e., total number of possible data subsets = rater groups = 36), weighting is needed.

3.3. EXAMPLES

In the current section, we illustrated the applications of the subdividing method using an operation dataset. The data analyzed came from a large-scale college level direct writing assessment in which each examinee (N = 5,905) responded to two essay prompts (i.e., items). Each response was evaluated by a pair of raters randomly selected from a pool of nine expert raters, resulting in a total of 23,620 ratings (5,905 examinees × 2 items × 2 raters). Ratings on this assessment were assigned on a six-point holistic scale. Approximately 73.6% and 25.9% of the ratings were in perfect agreement and adjacent agreement, respectively. Less than 1% of the ratings had a disagreement greater than one scale point. Because all examinees were scored by only a subset of raters from a large pool, the data set is sparse. We analyzed the data using the Subdividing method described in previous sections.

The sparsely filled data set with 23,630 ratings was parsed into small data subsets with either a *crossed*, *MBIB*, or *nested* design. Data subsets were analyzed only if they had a sample size of 12 or larger. Consequently, we analyzed 11 of the 16 *crossed* data sets found in the original data set, 32 of the 94 *nested* data sets, and 72 of the 125 *MBIB* data sets. We used 86.9% (20,524) of the total ratings, and no data were used more than once. A G study was performed on each of these data sets.

3.3.1. Variability Within Designs

Table 1A shows that the variance components for three of the *crossed* data sets chosen to be representative of the range of results obtained from the eleven *crossed* data sets. In each case, the $\hat{\sigma}^2_p$, $\hat{\sigma}^2_{pi}$, and $\hat{\sigma}^2_{pir,e}$ effects account for the greatest proportion of variance. The $\hat{\sigma}^2_i$ variance components are not as large, and the $\hat{\sigma}^2_r$, $\hat{\sigma}^2_{pr}$, and $\hat{\sigma}^2_{ir}$ components are negligible. However, there is considerable variability among these three *crossed* data sets. For example, the proportion of variance accounted by the $\hat{\sigma}^2_p$ effect ranged from 23% to 62% of the total variance. Such variability between subsets of the data emphasizes the risk associated with estimating variance components from only a sample of raters.

The columns under "All 11 Crossed Data Sets" (Table 1A) show the variance components averaged across all *crossed* data sets we analyzed. The relative magnitudes of the variance components associated with each effect are similar to those in the individual data sets. However, these averaged variance components are more accurate and stable estimates of the variance components for the entire data set.

Table B shows the estimated variance components for the three of the 72 *MBIB* data sets. These are chosen to represent the range of results obtained under this Subdividing method. As with the *crossed* data sets, the largest variance components are $\hat{\sigma}^2_p$, $\hat{\sigma}^2_{pi}$, and $\hat{\sigma}^2_{pir,e}$. The $\hat{\sigma}^2_i$ and $\hat{\sigma}^2_{pr}$ components are small and the $\hat{\sigma}^2_r$ and $\hat{\sigma}^2_{ir}$ terms are close to zero. There is a large amount of variability between the variance components obtained from the three example data sets for the *MBIB* designs (as was true for the *crossed* data sets). The columns under "All 72 MBIB Data Sets" (B) show the average variance components across all *MBIB* data sets. Again, these estimates should be more representative of the information contained in the entire data set than would be any single subset of the data. The averaged variance components are similar to those obtained from each of the individual *MBIB* data sets.

Table C shows the variance components for three of the 32 *nested* data sets. Compared to the other two designs, the *nested* design has more data sets of smaller size. Recall that only 32 of the 94 *nested* data sets contained 12 or more examinees (so that 62 of these data sets were excluded from our analyses). This is not surprising in operational settings in which random selection of four different raters is more efficient and convenient than systematically pairing up raters.

Due to the fact that raters are confounded within items, there is no way of estimating the unique effect for $\hat{\sigma}_r^2$, $\hat{\sigma}_{ir}^2$, and $\hat{\sigma}_{pr}^2$ in a *nested* design. This confounding allows estimations to be possible for only five variance components. Like the other two designs, the largest proportion of variance is accounted by $\hat{\sigma}_p^2$, $\hat{\sigma}_{pi}^2$, and $\hat{\sigma}_{pr:i,e}^2$ and the variability among the *nested* data sets is large. For example, the $\hat{\sigma}_p^2$ ranges from 11.33% to 65.71% of the total variance. The average variance components (Table 3C, rightmost side) are probably more representative of the entire data set than any other estimates from only a single subset.

Table 1: Variance Component Estimates for Subsets of Data of an Operational Data Set

A: Variance Components for Crossed Design Data Sets

Crossed	Data Set 1		Data Set 2		Data Set 3		All 11 Crossed Data Sets		
Source	VC	%	VC	%	VC	%	Mean VC	%	SD VC
Person (p)	0.3342	62.1	0.1277	36.8	0.0880	23.0	0.2023	44.2	0.07258
Item (i)	0.0095	1.8	0.0431	12.4	0.0283	7.4	0.0238	5.2	0.01648
Rater (r)	0.0004	0.1	0.0003	0.1	0.0041	1.1	0.0010	0.2	0.00313
Person x Item (pi)	0.0808	15.0	0.0798	23.0	0.1603	41.8	0.1117	24.4	0.03272
Person x Rater (pr)	0.0000	0.0	0.0053	1.5	0.0000	0.0	0.0105	2.3	0.01826
Item x Rater (ir)	0.0000	0.0	0.0018	0.5	0.0098	2.6	0.0018	0.4	0.00441
Person x Item x Rater, Error (pir,e)	0.1135	21.1	0.0890	25.7	0.0926	24.2	0.1070	23.4	0.02063

B: Variance Components for MBIB Design Data Sets

MBIB	Data Set 1		Data Set 2		Data Set 3		All 72 MBIB Data Sets		
Source	VC	%	VC	%	VC	%	Mean VC	%	SD VC
Person (p)	0.3045	45.5	0.3083	55.6	0.0664	25.2	0.2058	43.7	0.0815
Item (i)	0.0375	6.1	0.0013	0.2	0.0080	3.1	0.0190	4.0	0.0209
Rater (r)	0.0000	0.0	0.0000	0	0.0058	2.2	0.0000	0.0	0.0159
Person x Item (pi)	0.1300	19.7	0.1468	26.5	0.0371	14.1	0.1287	27.3	0.0502
Person x Rater (pr)	0.0000	0.0	0.0784	14.1	0.0432	16.4	0.0122	2.6	0.0455
Item x Rater (ir)	0.0086	1.5	0.0018	0.3	0.0000	0.0	0.0035	0.7	0.0183
Person x Item x Rater, Error (pir,e)	0.1760	27.3	0.0183	3.3	0.1027	39.0	0.1617	21.6	0.0569

C: Variance Components for Nested Design Data Sets

Nested	Data Set 1		Data Set 2		Data Set 3		All 32 Nested Data Sets		
Source	VC	%	VC	%	VC	%	Mean VC	%	SD VC
Person (p)	0.3605	65.7	0.2042	40.3	0.0362	11.3	0.1953	41.0	0.11890
Item (i)	0.0322	5.9	0.0000	0.0	0.0147	4.6	0.0327	6.8	0.06509
Rater:Item (r:i)	0.0000	0.0	0.0107	2.1	0.0207	6.5	0.0031	0.6	0.01004
Person x Item (pi)	0.0671	12.2	0.2196	43.3	0.1270	39.8	0.1352	28.3	0.07580
Person x (Rater:Item), Error (p(r:i))	0.0888	16.2	0.0726	14.3	0.1210	37.9	0.1107	23.	0.0313

Note: VC and % represent variance component and the percent of the total variance accounted for by the variance component. Mean VC is the average variance component, weighted by sample size, across all data sets within the same design. SD VC is the standard deviation of the variance components across data subsets. The average sample size for the Crossed, *MBIB*, and *Nested* designs are 109, 45, and 25, respectively.

3.3.2. Comparison Across Designs

Table 2A compares the average variance components for the *crossed* and *MBIB* data sets. The proportions of variance accounted for by each effect in these three designs were similar. Table 2B compares variance components from these three designs. For the *nested* design, the variance components for $\hat{\sigma}_p^2$ and $\hat{\sigma}_{pr:i,e}^2$ are slightly smaller, and the $\hat{\sigma}_i^2$ and $\hat{\sigma}_{pi}^2$ variance components are slightly larger than those of the *crossed* and *MBIB* designs. Table 2B also provides a summary of the pooled average across all the three deigns and shows that the $\hat{\sigma}_p^2$, $\hat{\sigma}_{pi}^2$, and $\hat{\sigma}_{pr:i,e}^2$ variance components were the three largest components.

Table 2: Aggregated Variance Component Estimates for an Operational Data Set

A: Averaged Components for Crossed and MBIB Subdividing Methods

	Crossed		MBIB	
Source	Mean VC	%	Mean VC	%
P	0.20230	44.2	0.20576	43.7
I	0.02381	5.2	0.01900	4.0
R	0.00100	0.2	0.00000	0.0
Pi	0.11168	24.4	0.12871	27.3
Pr	0.01052	2.3	0.01215	2.6
Ir	0.00176	0.4	0.00353	0.7
pir,e	0.10699	23.4	0.16167	21.6

B: Variance Components Averaged Across All Three Designs

	Crossed		MBIB		Nested		Average	
Source	VC	%	VC	%	VC	%	VC	%
Person (p)	0.20450	44.6	0.20580	43.8	0.19533	41.0	0.20389	43.5
Item (i)	0.02346	5.1	0.01900	4.0	0.03270	6.8	0.02206	4.7
Rater:Item (r:i)	0.00278	0.6	0.00281	0.6	0.00308	0.6	0.00285	0.6
Person x Item (pi)	0.11050	24.1	0.12871	27.4	0.13516	28.3	0.12582	26.8
Person x (Rater:Item), Error (p(r:i))	0.11690	25.5	0.11382	24.2	0.11070	23.2	0.11340	24.3

Though the above operational dataset can illustrate the subdividing method, we do not know the extent to which it can be used in other datasets. A simulation can be used to address this question. In succeeding sections, I described an experimental study to evaluate the statistical properties of the subdividing method. Specifically, I first stated the research questions then described the independent variables and the dependent variables to address those questions. A review of the measurement literature guided the choices of the population values manipulated in the independent variables, which reflected realistic scoring situations in large-scale assessment programs.

3.4. EVALUATION OF THE SUBDIVIDING METHOD

3.4.1. Research Questions

What is the performance of the subdividing method? The answers to research questions one through eight in Table 3 are addressed in the light of the accuracy and precision of variance components. The amount of missing data is manifested by the size of a rater pool and the volume of performance-based tasks to be scored. The pattern of missing data is manifested by the rating plan used to score the examinees. The certainty of a decision can be evaluated by examining the accuracy and stability of the estimated variance components and composite indices. The reliability and the dependability of a scoring procedure are represented by the ρ^2 and ϕ coefficients, respectively. To what extent do the amounts and patterns of unbalanced data influence the certainty of judging the measurement errors, reliability, and dependability of a scoring procedure? Research questions four through eight in Table 3 address these questions.

Table 3 : Research Questions

Research Questions	Rationales and Significance
1) How did weighting influence the G theory estimates?	How does the use of weighting schemes to combine the variance components influence the accuracy and stability of the estimates of the variance-component and the composite indices? When do data subsets need to be weighted? What are the situations in which weighting can be ignored? What are the consequences of not using weights when they should be used?
2) What was the effect of doubling the batch size?	A batch contains a number of examinees whose performances are scored by a common group of raters. How well can the subdividing method recover the population value of the variance components and generalizability coefficients when the "batch size" changes? Will doubling the batch size (i.e., from 12 to 24) increase the accuracy and precision of the variance components estimates?
3) How accurately did the subdividing method recover variance components and composite indices?	Both the variance components and composite indices are critical in determining the quality of measurement procedures. How accurate can the subdividing method recover the parameter values of variance components and composite indices?
4) How well did the subdividing method estimate the item effect?	Increasing the sample size of one facet has an effect on just that facet itself when one uses ordinary algorithms such as ANOVA, MINQUE, ML, and REML methods. To what degree does the subdividing method have the properties that ordinary algorithms have? Specifically, when one increases the number of raters used and examinees tested, it should have little to do with the *item* effect. Does this property hold for the subdividing method?

Research Questions	Rationales and Significance
5) What was the effect of expanding the size of the rater pool?	Increasing the rater pool size, on the one hand, gives more information about the degree to which raters score examinees differently. It, on the other hand, causes more unobserved data because no matter how large the rater pool size, only a random pair of rater is chosen to score an examinee. To what degree does the expansion of the rater pool increase the precision of the estimation of rater-related measurement errors, in unbalanced situations? How do the two factors (rater pool size and amounts of missing data) influence the *person-by-rater* effect? Will the increase in the rater pool size compensate for the increase in the amount of missing data?
6) Can the subdividing method handle a large volume of examinees? How well did it perform?	Frequently, large-scale testing programs score a tremendous volume of examinees and it is infeasible to have all raters score all examinees. Given the large amounts of data and the sparse nature of the data structure in these testing programs, can the subdividing method handle the data? If so, how well does it perform?
7) What were the advantages and disadvantages of the two rating plans?	To what extent does the *disconnected crossed* rating plan provide better estimates than the *connected mixture* rating plan? In the *connected mixture* rating plan, only a portion of the data is allocated to estimate the rater related effects such as the *person-by-rater* effect; how precisely are these effects estimated? How do these estimates compare to those in the *disconnected crossed* rating plan?
8) How did the amounts and pattern of missing data influence the norm- and criterion- referenced indices?	In addition to variance components, generalizability coefficients and misclassification rates are used for making decisions regarding the overall quality of a measurement procedure. How do the amounts and patterns of missing data influence these composite indices, namely the generalizability coefficient, dependability coefficient, and the misclassification rate?

3.5. CONDITIONS TO VARY

3.5.1. Summary of All Conditions

Table 4 shows the conditions used to evaluate performance of the subdividing method. The simulation study entailed the following factors, resulting in 176 conditions.

- Rating plans (2 levels)
- Number of examinees (4 levels)
- Number of raters (3 levels for the 750-, 1500-, and 3000- examinee conditions and 2 levels for the 6000-examinee-condition)
- Variation in item difficulty (2 levels)
- Rater inconsistency (2 levels)
- Number of essays in a batch (2 levels)

Table 4: Experimental Conditions to Evaluate the Subdividing Method

Experimental Conditions			High Item Effect (σ^2_i)				Low Item Effect (σ^2_i)			
			High rater inconsistency (σ^2_{pr})		Low rater inconsistency (σ^2_{pr})		High rater inconsistency (σ^2_{pr})		Low rater inconsistency (σ^2_{pr})	
	N examinees	N raters	12 essays per batch	24 essays per batch	12 essays per batch	24 essays per batch	12 essays per batch	24 essays per batch	12 essays per batch	24 essays per batch
Disconnected Crossed Rating Plans	750	2								
		4								
		8								
	1500	4								
		8								
		14								
	3000	8								
		14								
		28								
	6000	14								
		28								
Mixture of Connected Rating Plans	750	2								
		4								
		8								
	1500	4								
		8								
		14								
	3000	8								
		14								
		28								
	6000	14								
		28								

Note: The numbers of raters reported indicate the number of raters needed to complete the scoring session in 40, 20, and 10 days, respectively. It is assumed that examinees respond to two items and each item is scored twice by two different raters and it takes 10 minutes to read an essay and all raters work 7.5 hours a day. Consequently, it will take 40 days to score when a low volume of raters (i.e., 2, 4, 8,8, 14) is recruited for each N examinees value. The scoring time will decrease by 50% when a medium rater pool is employed (i.e., 4, 8, 14, & 28). It takes only 10 days when a large pool of raters is recruited (i.e., 8, 14, & 28). A rater pool size of 4 is considered medium when it is used to score 750 examinees, but it is considered low when is used to score 1500 examinees. The same rule applies to other size of rater pools.

3.5.2. Rater Severity and Inconsistencies

Rater severity and rater inconsistencies are reflected in the variance components (σ^2_r, σ^2_{pr}, σ^2_{ir}, and σ^2_{ir}). Longford (1995, pages 21-2) defined σ^2_r as the *rater severity* and σ^2_{pr} as the *rater inconsistency* in a one facet person-by-rater model. I have adopted his definition for σ^2_r and elaborated his definition of *rater inconsistency* to distinguish the two types of *rater consistency* in a two facet model. Specifically, I define σ^2_{pr} as the effect for *person-by-rater inconsistency*, σ^2_{ir} as *item-by-rater inconsistency*, and σ^2_{pir} as *idiosyncratic inconsistency*. Rater severity ($\sigma^2_r = \underset{r}{E}(\mu_r - \mu)^2$) refers to the expected variation in a random rater's mean score μ_r (over the population of examinees and items) about the mean score of all raters μ (mean over the populations of examinees, items, and raters). So, a large rater severity effect indicates that the mean scores were different between raters and thus some raters were more lenient or harsh than the others. Research has repeatedly found that rater severity is almost negligible across many different types of assessments (e.g., Brennan, 1995, a writing test; Shavelson, 1993, a science test), given that sufficient training and monitoring is provided to raters (Cronbach et al., 1994; Koretz et al., 1994; Patz, 1996; Wainer, 1993).

I varied the magnitude of the *person-by-rater inconsistency* effect in the simulation because it has important implications to fair assessment in scoring (Do the raters score examinees differently averaged across items?). Since *rater severity* has been shown to be universally so small that it can be neglected, it was practical to hold it constant and manipulate person-by-rater inconsistency in the simulations.

Table 5 shows a summary of the variance components reported in four published studies involving human judgements. The third column indicates the scoring scale employed in the studies. As the studies employed a different scoring scale (a 6-point scale on the first two studies and 5-point scale on the last two), it was necessary to use a common metric (relative percent of variation based on the total variation) to compare the variance components. The mean percent of total variation for *person-by-rater inconsistency* (mean $\sigma^2_{pr} = 3\%$) was both larger and more variable than that for rater severity (mean $\sigma^2_r < 1\%$).

Table 5: Summary of Variance Component Magnitudes in the Literature

Authors	Year	Subjects	Scoring Scale	Total Variation	Person P	Item I	Rater R	PI	PR	IR	PIR, E
Brennan et al.	1995	Writing	0 to 5	1.15967	59%	2%	1%	14%	4%	1%	19%
Chiu et al.	1997	Writing	1 to 6	0.47281	41%	5%	0%	25%	4%	1%	23%
Lane et al.	1996	Math	0 to 4	1.84215	25%	11%	0%	53%	0%	0%	10%
Linn et al.	1996	Math	0 to 4	1.01500	20%	22%	0%	33%	1%	2%	21%
			Average	**0.96331**	**35%**	**11%**	**0%**	**31%**	**3%**	**1%**	**20%**

3.5.3. Examinees

Large-scale assessments can have numbers of examinees ranging from a few hundred to several thousand, or even tens of thousands for state and national tests. Longford (1995) reported that 3,756 examinees responded to the Studio Art Portfolio Assessment and Myford, Marr, and Linacre (1995) reported 5,400 examinees took the Test of Written English (TWE) in one administration. Chiu and Wolfe (1997) stated that 5,905 examinees participated in an administration of the Collegiate Assessment of Academic Proficiency (CAAP). Lane, Liu, Ankenmann, and Stone (1996) conducted generalizability analyses on 2,514 examinees who had responded to all the tasks in the QUASAR Cognitive Assessment Instrument (QCAI).

3.5.4. Item Sampling

Data were simulated to model a case with two items and two ratings per item. This choice reflects the common practice in examinations where essay writing was involved (e.g., Collegiate Assessment of Academic Proficiency or CAAP, Graduate Management Admission Test or GMAT, and Medical College Admission Test or MCAT). Each item was scored two times (occasions) by completely different raters.

3.5.5. Size of Rater Pool

The size of the rater pool was varied to reflect practical situations. In the study by Lane, Liu, Ankenmann, and Stone (1996), 34 raters were hired to score the QCAI examinations of 2,514 examinees. In another study by Chiu and Wolfe (1997), nine raters were used to score 5,905 examinees. The two examples (Lane et al., 1996 and Chiu & Wolfe, 1997) show that the number of examinees and the size of the pool of raters need not be in direct proportion. Many other intervening operational factors influence this functional relationship. Such factors include the *number of tasks answered by an examinee, number of ratings on each task, total number of days available for scoring, time (in minutes) it takes to score a task*, and *average work hours per rater per day*. Appendix G shows an equation to determine the number of raters needed to complete the scoring of an examination for varying sample sizes, while holding constant the other operational factors.

3.5.6. Amounts and Patterns of Missing Data

To test the robustness of the subdividing method, I modeled a practical situation in which the pattern of missing data was contingent on the measurement procedure. Changing the size of a hypothetical rater pool while holding constant the number of times a task was rated changed the amount of missing data. If five examinees were crossed with four raters, the number of possible ratings per item is 20 (5 examinees x 4 raters). However, if one randomly chooses only a pair of raters out of the pool of four raters, the number of possible ratings reduces to 10 (5 x 2), which is 50% of the total available ratings if all four raters were used (20). The other half of the ratings would be missing because they were unobserved by design. The percent of unobserved data increases further as the rater pool size expands to six raters. Here using a pair of raters resulted in 66.6% of all possible data being unobserved (10 ratings of 30 possible are observed). The proportion of missing data increases as the size of the rater pool increases, holding constant the number of ratings each examinee received. The current study manipulated the rater pool size to investigate the effects of amounts and patterns of missing data on the accuracy and precision of the subdividing method.

3.5.7. Rating Plans

Frequently, raters work in groups during scoring sessions (Clauser, Clyman, and Swanson, 1999). The decision to group raters determines the nature of the unbalanced data patterns in generalizability analyses and these decisions are referred to as "rating plans" throughout the current book. How many rater groups can a rater sit in? Are the raters required to score all tasks or just one task submitted by an examinee? How many times is an examinee scored for each task submitted? How flexible are the rules used to assign examinees and tasks to raters? Despite the fact that these decisions are indispensable in setting up scoring procedures in operational settings, they are seldom written or published.

Using the rating plans employed by Brennan, Gao, and Colton (1995), Chiu and Wolfe (1997), Lane et al. (1996), Linn et al. (1996), Gordon, (1998),

Vickers (1998), and Welch (1996), four principles that characterize rating plans, listed in Table 6 (p. 48), were deduced. With these principles, two basic rating plans were examined in the current monograph, namely the *disconnected crossed* rating plan and the *connected mixture* rating plan.

Disconnected crossed rating plan

The *disconnected crossed* rating plan has often been used for research purposes, and entails rigorous rules for setting up scoring procedures (e.g., Brennan, Gao, Colton, 1995). An example of the *disconnected crossed* rating plan follows. Prior to staring to the scoring, raters were grouped and each group would be expected to score the same number of examinees. In this arrangement, raters work *within* rather than *across* groups — all members in the same group score all the items / tasks submitted by all examinees assigned to the group. This scenario was referred to as "disconnected", as there were no common raters sitting in two groups (Engelhard, 1996 and Searle, 1987). The merit of this setup is the capability of accumulating a large amount of data for each group for subsequent generalizability analysis. The *disconnected crossed* rating plan is frequently adapted when the volume of examinees is manageable to manipulate the ways of assigning examinees and tasks to raters, assuming the assignment is implemented manually rather than electronically (storing the tasks on digital formats and use computers to assign the task to raters).

Regarding this *disconnected crossed* rating plan, researchers have studied whether raters were aware of their membership in a group and whether raters were allowed to discuss the scoring process (e.g., Clauser, Swanson, & Clyman, 1996). For this research study, no assumption was made concerning rater discussions. As much as raters might be aware of their membership in the *disconnected crossed* rating plan, they are not necessarily aware of the group they belong to because the group membership may be decided as a post hoc or a random process. For instance, portfolios may be grouped in advance and one rater assigned to score those portfolios once. Another rater may be chosen at random, without noticing or knowing of the first rater, to assign a second rating to the same set of portfolios. Although the two raters did not know with whom they worked, they are considered to belong to the same group as they scored the same set of portfolios from the same examinees. This is a "crossed" rating plan as raters in a group are instructed to score all the tasks submitted by examinees assigned to the group. Figure 4 depicts a sample *disconnected crossed* rating plan using a hypothetical data set with a pool of four raters scoring two items for and 50 examinees. Each "X" represents a test score assigned by a rater to an examinee on an item. Cells without an "X" indicate missing or unobserved data.

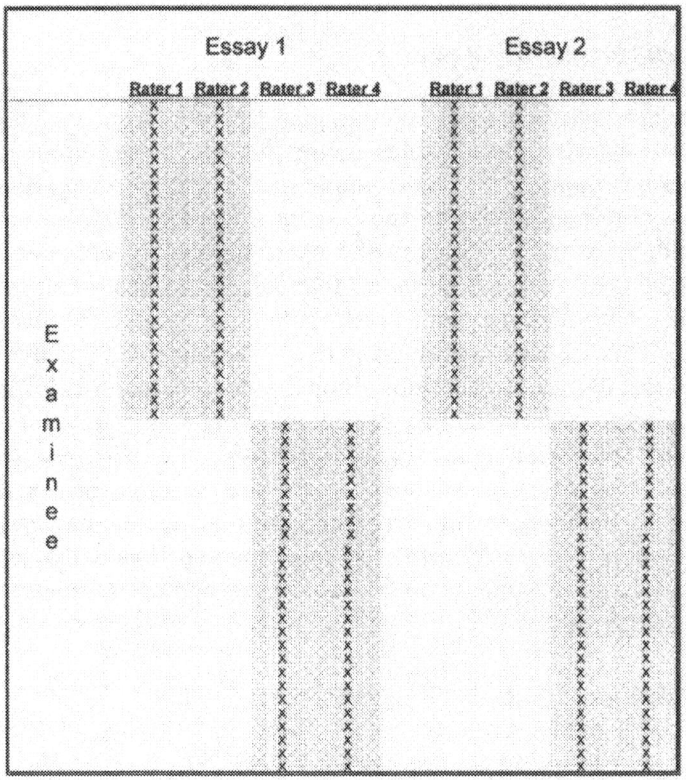

Figure 4: A hypothetical data set illustrating the *disconnected crossed* rating plan.

Connected mixture rating plan

The *connected mixture* rating plan is frequently used when the volume of examinees is large and it is more cost-effective and convenient to use a random process than to impose rigorous rules guiding the rater-task-examinee assignments. For instance, an examinee's tasks might be organized in a portfolio (containing tasks submitted by the same examinee), which would then be mixed with other examinees' portfolios for raters to select at random. Once a rater had selected a portfolio, s/he scored one or more tasks in that portfolio. Whether or not the rater scored all the tasks in a portfolio (denoted as a *crossed* structural design) may depend on convenience, guidelines suggested by scoring centers, the nature of the examination, and expertise of the rater. Although tasks are more likely to be scored according to raters' expertise in a highly specialized examination than in, for instance, a language arts writing exam, variations exist regarding the number and nature of tasks in a portfolio scored by a rater. Raters may be instructed to score an essay in a portfolio and then return it so that another rater can be randomly selected for scoring the other essay in the same portfolio (denoted as a *nested* structural design). If one rater works with one other rater on a first essay and then works with another rater on a second essay, this leads to the *MBIB* structural design mentioned in the *Modeling Stage* on page 20.

Unlike the *disconnected crossed* rating plan in which raters were usually grouped prior to the starting of scoring, the idea of forming groups in this rating plan is less conspicuous — raters do not usually know who they will work with. Due to the random process used for the rater-task-examinee assignment, with this plan raters have the opportunity to work with more raters than they could in the *disconnected crossed* rating plan. Raters are "connected" in this rating plan because their ratings are compared directly or indirectly through other raters. Figure 5 on page 48 shows a hypothetical data set illustrating the *connected mixture* rating plan with two essays, four raters, and 50 examinees. By examining which raters were chosen to score an examinee, one can observe that the hypothetical data set contains three structural designs, namely the *crossed*, *MBIB*, and *nested* designs (these designs are separated by two horizontal lines in the figure).

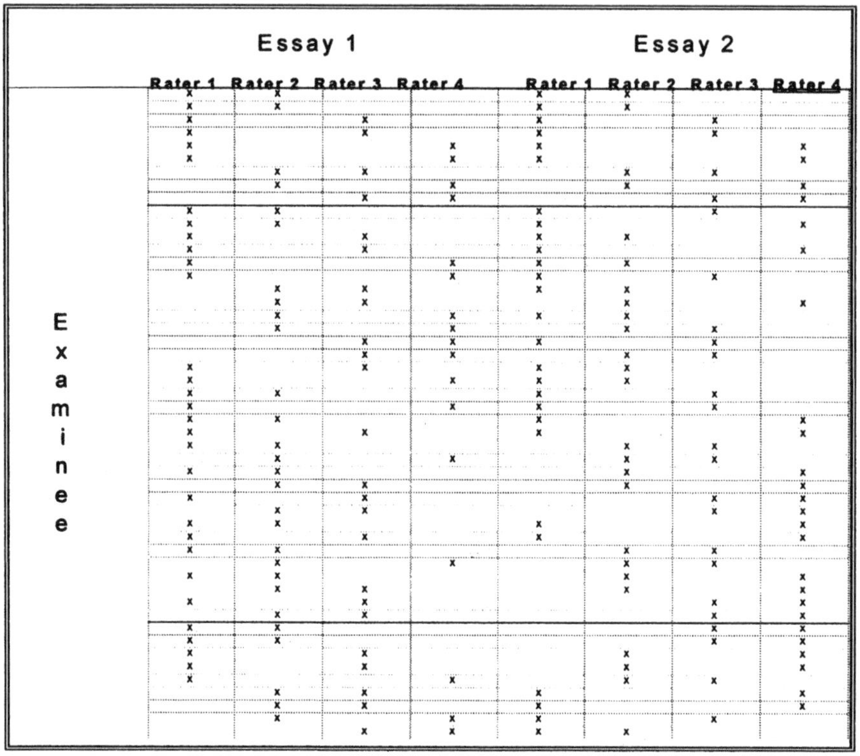

Figure 5: A hypothetical data set illustrating the *connected mixture* rating plan.

In practice, different versions of the two rating plans introduced in the above section were adopted in various scoring centers (Gordon, 1998; Vickers, 1998) and the principles shown in Table 6 capture the essentials.

Table 6: Principles of Rating Plans

Principles	Disconnected crossed plan	Connected mixture plan
1. Number of ratings on each task for a given examinee	2	2
2. Linking between groups	raters belong to only one group	no restriction
3. Guiding structural designs within a given group	limited to only the crossed design	no limitation; structural design could be crossed, nested, and other designs
4. Number of examinees scored by groups of raters.	planned; every group of raters scores the same number of examinees.	unplanned; groups may or may not score the same number of examinees depending on the size of rater pool and sample size.

3.5.8. Batch Size

The procedure used to assign tasks to raters was called task assignment. In addition to randomly assigning essays to raters, scoring centers (e.g., Georgia State Department of Education and ACT, Inc.) often impose rules for the scoring procedures to accommodate operational needs. An important dimension of setting up a rating plan is to arrange essays so that they can be efficiently graded. For example, rather than randomly assigning every essay to each rater, scoring centers often organize essays in batches (Gordon, 1998; Schafer, 1998; Vickers, 1998; Welch, 1996; Wolfe, 1998). Those batches can be randomly assigned to groups of raters. Packing essays in batches saves operational time because it takes more time for raters to exchange single essays than a batch of essays. Packing essays in bundles also controls the number of essays to be scored by a common group of raters. Bundling also structures ratings for reliability analysis -- without the bundling of essays, the data set may be too sparsely-filled to conduct an analysis.

3.6. DATA GENERATION

3.6.1. Linear Model

A total of 17,600 balanced data sets were generated, 100 sets for each the 176 conditions under the specification of a two-faceted balanced design (Schroeder, 1982, p.36), namely the *person x item x rater* design specified in Appendix A. The score X_{pir} of any given observation in this model was expressed as a sum of seven components,

$$X_{pir} = x_p + x_i + x_r + x_{pi} + x_{pr} + x_{ir} + x_{pir,e.} \qquad (14)$$

Each of the seven components were generated under a normal distribution $x_a \sim (0, \sigma_a^2)$, where $\sigma_a^2 = \{\sigma_p^2 = 0.3;\ \sigma_i^2 = 0.02$ (low), 0.11 (high); $\sigma_r^2 = 0.01;\ \sigma_{pi}^2 = 0.30;\ \sigma_{pr}^2 = 0.01$ (low), 0.1 (high); $\sigma_{ir}^2 = 0.01$; and $\sigma_{pir,e}^2 = 0.20$). For example, the score for person *p*, responding to item *i*, judged by rater *r*, was the sum of seven random numbers each generated independently from the above seven normal distributions. Table 7 shows the population values of the variance components and the values of the corresponding composite population indices.

Table 7: Population Parameters for the Variance Components and Composites

Crossed and MBIB Designs		High Item Effect: High Rater Inconsistency Effect	High Item Effect: Low Rater Inconsistency Effect	Low Item Effect: High Rater Inconsistency Effect	Low Item Effect: Low Rater Inconsistency Effect
Variance Components	p	0.35	0.35	0.35	0.35
	i	0.11	0.11	0.02	0.02
	r	0.01	0.01	0.01	0.01
	pi	0.30	0.30	0.30	0.30
	pr	0.10	0.01	0.10	0.01
	ir	0.01	0.01	0.01	0.01
	pir	0.20	0.20	0.20	0.20
Composites	Standard Error of Measurement (Relative)	0.50000	0.45277	0.50000	0.45277
	Standard Error of Measurement (Absolute)	0.55902	0.51720	0.51720	0.47170
	Generalizability Coefficient	0.58333	0.63063	0.58333	0.63063
	Dependability Coefficient	0.52830	0.56680	0.56680	0.61135
	Misclassification Error	0.03682	0.02659	0.02659	0.01700

3.6.2. Observed Score Scale

The observed scores X_{pir} were the sums of the scores of the seven effects in (14). The sums would have a mean of 0 and standard deviation of approximately one indicating that roughly 99.9% of the scores should be between –3 and 3. If 3 were added to all scores, the total scores would approximate scores on a seven-point scale ranging from 0 to 6 with a mean 3 and standard deviation of 1.

3.6.3. Score Scale Truncation

In practice, test scores for performance assessment are often assigned as integer scores (e.g., 1, 2, …, 6) with an underlying discrete distribution. Much research, however, has employed the normal distribution or other continuous distributions for research purposes (e.g., Brennan, Harris, and Hanson, 1987; Bost, 1995; and Smith, 1992). Longford (1995) examined the effect of using normal scores as opposed to integer scores when using simulations to examine the accuracy and precision of estimated variance components. Using a one-faceted model (person-by-rater), Longford simulated 200 trials with test scores generated from a normal distribution. He then compared the estimated variance components obtained from the normal distribution with those obtained by truncating the fractional scores to integers. Longford concluded that the bias due to the truncated scores is somewhat greater than that for the estimator for the 'normal' scores, but the difference in bias was unimportant. The following reported the results found in Longford's comparison (Longford, 1995, pp. 43 - 45).

Table 8: Comparison Between Normal and Rounded Scores

	Normal Scores			Rounded Scores		
	σ^2_p	σ^2_r	$\sigma^2_{pr,e}$	σ^2_p	σ^2_r	$\sigma^2_{pr,e}$
True value	0.730	0.062	0.370	0.730	0.062	0.371
Mean	0.749	0.077	0.350	0.722	0.074	0.421
Std. deviation	(0.067)	(0.038)	(0.040)	(0.065)	(0.038)	(0.041)

3.6.4. Missing Data Generation

Following the generation of the balanced data sets, sparsely filled data sets were created. This was accomplished by randomly deleting scores from the balanced data sets. The sparse patterns were modeled to reflect the unbalanced patterns appearing in the two rating plans (see Appendix I for programming code).

Disconnected crossed **rating plan**

The following three rules were employed to generate data for the *disconnected crossed* rating plan.

$$t = crossed \tag{15}$$

$$rater_{i,t,s} \neq rater'_{i,t,s} \tag{16}$$

$$rater_{t,s} \neq rater_{t,s'} \tag{17}$$

The rule listed in Equation (16) ensured that no single rater score an examinee on the same item (i) twice in a given data subset (s) of the *crossed* design. The last rule, in Equation (17), required that every rater participate in the scoring of only one data subset. In Equation (15), only the *crossed* design appears implying that the raters who scored one item for an examinee also scored the other item and that the same raters scored all the examinees in a data subset (s).

***Connected mixture* rating plan**

Regarding this rating plan, only the second rule, equation (16), applied to the data generation procedure. The third rule was not imposed on this rating plan so that raters could participate in scoring more than just one data subset. Whether or not they participated in more than one data subset was a random process. When raters participated in more than one data subset, they provided a link between the subsets they scored and for this reason, the current rating plan was referred to as "connected". The first rule was amended so that

$$t = crossed, MBIB, nested. \qquad (18)$$

Because raters scored either just one item or both items for a given examinee in a data subset, this arrangement allowed a data subset to exhibit either a *crossed*, *MBIB*, and *nested* structure and so this rating plan was referred to as a mixture of structural designs.

3.6.5. Negative Variance Components

Variance component estimates can be negative because of many reasons discussed in Brennan (1992), Cronbach, Gleser, Nanda, Rajaratnam (1972), Marcoulides (1987), and Searle, Casella, and McCulloch (1992). Some reasons are: (a) The population values are indeed zero or close to zero; (b) Insufficient data are used to estimate the variance components; (c) The model is misspecified; and (d) The estimation procedure is incorrect. Brennan (1992, p.48) suggested one examine possible reasons contributing to the occurrence of negative variance components and asserted that setting negative estimates to zero resulted in biased estimates. Because unbiased estimates were desirable, negative variance components were set to zero for reporting, but their negative values were used in all computational procedures for composite indices.

3.7. OUTCOMES AND DATA ANALYSIS

3.7.1. Outcomes

Two performance measures of the estimators produced by the subdividing method were examined. *Accuracy* indicated the degree to which the average of an estimator departs from its population value. *Precision* indicated the variability of an estimator. Both criteria were important for the estimates of the variance-components and the composite indices because how well the estimators perform on these criteria affects high-stakes decisions made based on G theory. The estimates and the true parameter values for variance components, the generalizability coefficient, dependability coefficient, and misclassification rates were examined using the *Accuracy* and *Precision* measures, which were summarized as follows.

3.7.2. Accuracy, Bias, and Precision

The Mean Square Error (MSE) indicates the squared loss, or the averaged square difference between an estimator and its known population value. Harwell et al. (1996) and Othman (1995) used this index to evaluate the quality of an estimator. This index comprised two components, namely the squared bias and the variance (see the following relations).

$$\mathrm{MSE} = \frac{\sum_{j=1}^{e}(\hat{\theta}_j - \theta)^2}{e}$$

$$= (\bar{\hat{\theta}} - \theta)^2 + \frac{\sum_{j=1}^{e}(\hat{\theta}_j - \bar{\hat{\theta}})^2}{e}$$

$$= \text{Squared Bias} + \text{Variance} \qquad (19)$$

The $\hat{\theta}_j$ in (19) represents the G theory estimate from the jth trial; θ is the known population parameter, representing true values for the variance components and composites; e is the number of trials of each simulation (i.e., 100); and $\bar{\hat{\theta}}$ is the mean of $\hat{\theta}_j$ over the e trials. Ideally, a zero MSE would indicate that the subdividing method provided an estimate identical to its population value. A low MSE is desirable because it indicates very little bias and variability of an estimate. A large MSE is less desirable and can be contributed to by either or both a large variance and a large bias. To disentangle these two sources of errors in estimation, researchers (e.g., Marcoulides, 1988; Othman, 1995) have reported variance and bias as two separate indices, and it is a common practice to modify these two indices so that they become more meaningful and easy to interpret.

Standard Errors (inverse of precision)

The square root of the variance in (19) equaled the empirical standard error used to examine the variability of the estimators produced by the subdividing method. The standard error was computed by obtaining the standard deviation of an estimator in a simulation. The inverse of the square root of variance was referred to as "precision", which was used interchangeably with standard error to describe the variability of the G theory estimates in the current study. A precise estimate has low variance (or standard error) and an imprecise estimate has high variance.

Accuracy (measure of bias)

Accuracy of a simulation can be measured in many ways and one lucid way was to express accuracy as a percentage. Technically, it was measured as the average ratio between an estimate and the parameter value of that estimate across all replications. Computationally, accuracy is defined as:

$$\text{Accuracy} = \frac{1}{e}\sum_{j=1}^{e}\frac{\hat{\theta}_j}{\theta}. \tag{20}$$

The above index treated all discrepancies between the estimators to their population values equally serious. An accuracy equals one indicates that the estimates were recovered perfectly; whereas an accuracy higher than one indicates overestimation and yet an accuracy lower than one indicates underestimation.

3.7.3. Empirical Versus Theoretical Standard Errors (SEs)

Standard errors based on asymptotic assumptions (Brennan, 1992, pp. 133-135; Burdick & Graybill, 1992) can be inaccurate because the degree to which the SE reflects the sampling distribution of a variance component depends upon factors like sample size, normality, and the amounts and patterns of missing data involved. In addition to relying on assumptions that were difficult to satisfy in the current data, Brennan (1992) and Burdick and Graybill (1992) did not discuss how to estimate or compute a SE when multiple samples were available. According to Brennan (1992), the theoretical SEs for the variance components are functions of the mean squares of the facets and their degrees of freedom. The matrix notation for the theoretical standard error was summarized in Equation (6) and the formulae are given in terms of variance components and sample sizes in Appendix B. The theoretical standard errors reported in the Results section were based on the formula in Appendix B, computed using two raters. the value two was chosen because a random pair of raters was selected to score each examinee, even though more than two raters were available in the pool. These standard errors were compared to the empirical standard errors to investigate how precisely variance components were recovered over the 100 replications.

3.7.4. Empirical Versus Theoretical Confidence Intervals (CI)

The skewed distribution (due to low *df* in a χ^2 distribution) of the variance components can cause their CI to be asymmetrical; that is, the two sides of the CI have unequal lengths (e.g., a hypothetical 95% CI for a variance-component estimate of 0.45 could be [0.40, 0.60]). Brennan (1992) and Burdick and Graybill (1992) developed methods to construct CIs for variance components under balanced designs but not for unbalanced designs. Nor did they develop methods to construct CIs for composite indices.

To construct an empirical 95% CI for a variance component, I used the observed variance components at the 2.5^{th} and 97.5^{th} percentiles of each of the seven simulated distributions. The theoretical 95% CI was computed by multiplying the standard error by a correction factor reported in Brennan (1992, Table D.1). The 95% empirical CI for the composites was computed by first obtaining the composites based on the synthesized variance components followed by reporting the composites at the 2.5^{th} and the 97.5^{th} percentiles of the composites.

Gao (1992) suggested that one use the upper and lower limits of the absolute standard error of measurement and those of the universe score variance to compute the theoretical CI for the composites. The upper limit of the CI for composites was computed by dividing the upper bound of the universe score variance by the sum of itself and lower bound of the absolute standard error of measurement. For instance, the upper limit of the generalizability coefficient is defined as

$$E\hat{\rho}^2_{upper} = \frac{\hat{\sigma}^2_{p_{upper}}}{\hat{\sigma}^2_{p_{upper}} + \hat{\sigma}^2_{\delta_{lower}}}, \tag{21}$$

where
$$\hat{\sigma}^2_{\delta_{lower}} = \frac{\hat{\sigma}^2_{pi_{lower}}}{n'_i} + \frac{\hat{\sigma}^2_{pr_{lower}}}{n'_r} + \frac{\hat{\sigma}^2_{pir,e_{lower}}}{n'_i n'_r}. \tag{22}$$

Likewise, the lower limit of a 95% theoretical CI for the composites was obtained by dividing the lower bound of the universe score variance by the sum of this variance and the upper bound of the absolute standard error of measurement

$$E\hat{\rho}^2_{lower} = \frac{\hat{\sigma}^2_{p_{lower}}}{\hat{\sigma}^2_{p_{lower}} + \hat{\sigma}^2_{\delta_{upper}}}. \tag{23}$$

Chapter 4
VALIDATIONS OF THE SUBDIVIDING METHOD

As described in the previous chapter, the volume of examinees, number of raters, and examinee- and task- to-rater assignment determined the amounts and patterns of missing data and thus influence the estimation of measurement errors. How does each of these factors impact the precision of individual variance components (measurement errors for scoring performance-based assessments)? How can one use the subdividing method to alleviate the potential inaccuracy and imprecision caused by unbalanced data? Which variance components are influenced by the increase in sample size, and which variance components are influenced by the expansion of rater pool size? These questions are central to this chapter.

Section 4.1 examines the effect of using weights when synthesizing variance components. Section 4.2 compares the measurement errors estimated from data generated by different missing data mechanisms, namely using a small batch size (12 examinees) versus a large batch size (24 examinees). Section 4.3 summarizes data on accuracy of the subdividing method and sections 4.4 through 4.6 summarize data on the precision of the subdividing method. Section 4.7 compares and contrasts the two rating plans (*disconnected crossed* and *connected mixture*) in the light of the precision of variance components and section 4.8 covers the performance of the subdividing on the generalizability coefficient, dependability coefficient, and misclassification errors. The composite indices are discussed in the context of the *disconnected crossed* rating plan as it utilized a larger amount of data than did the *connected mixture* rating plan, for the analysis of a completely crossed *person-by-rater-by-item* design. Table 9 on provides an overview of the results reported in the subsequent sections, obtained from the simulation with 100 replications.

Table 9 : Table of Major Findings

Research Questions	Results
1) How did weighting influence the G theory estimates?	Weighting had no effect on the variance components estimated in the *disconnected crossed* rating plan. It increased the precision of variance component estimates in the *connected mixture* rating plan when the data subsets differed in size.
2) What was the effect of doubling the batch size?	Using a batch size of 24 did not have any noticeable effects on the accuracy and precision of the variance components and composite indices in both rating plans.
3) How accurately did the subdividing method recover variance components and composite indices?	The variance components and composites were recovered with accuracy close to 100% in both rating plans.
4) How well did the subdividing method estimate the *item* effect?	The subdividing method estimated *item* effects in the way they should be estimated using ordinary algorithms in balanced designs. Increasing the size of rater pool or the sample size did not change the accuracy and precision of the *item* effect.
5) What was the effect of expanding the size of the rater pool?	Increasing the rater pool reduced the standard error of the *rater* and *item-by-rater* effects in the *disconnected crossed* rating plan and the *rater-nested-in-item* effect in the *connected mixture* rating plan.
6) Can the subdividing method handle a large volume of examinees? How well did it perform?	(a) The subdividing method can always handle more examinees than any other methods that analyze the entire data set all at once. As long as one can partition a sparsely data set into subsets with manageable sizes, there is no restriction on the size of the sparsely filled data set. (b) The larger the volume of the examinees, the more precisely the following effects were estimated: *person*, *person-by-item*, *person-by-rater*, and *person-by-item-by-rater* effects.

7) What were the advantages and disadvantages of the two rating plans?	For a universe of generalization exhibiting a $p \times I \times R$ design, the *disconnected crossed* rating plan requires tremendous amount of efforts to route tasks to raters but it provided precise estimates for the rater-related effects; whereas the *connected mixture* rating plan did not provided precise rater-related estimates although it requires less effort for routing. The *connected mixture* rating plan, however, can yield precise rater-related estimates for a universe of generalization exhibiting a $p \times R : I$ design.
8) How did the amounts and pattern of missing data influence the norm- and criterion- referenced indices?	All composite indices were estimated as accurately and precisely as they should be estimated in balanced situations in both rating plans. Subsampling different pairs of raters to score different groups of examinees provided confidence intervals parallel to using the same pair of raters to score all examinees.

4.1. COMPARISON OF POOLED RESULTS WITH WEIGHTS AND WITHOUT WEIGHTS

4.1.1. Precision (Inverse of Standard Errors)

Weighting data subsets by sample size recovered very closely the theoretical standard error when the data subsets differed in sample size. Data subsets differed by sample size occurred in only two conditions (first condition: $n_{p\bullet\bullet}$=750 and $n_{r\bullet\bullet}$=4; second condition: $n_{p\bullet\bullet}$=1500 and $n_{r\bullet\bullet}$=4) where the rater pool size had four raters in the *connected mixture* rating plan. Figure 6 through Figure 11 on pages 61 to 63 show the precision of the three variance components interacting with the object of measurement (person), namely $\hat{\sigma}^2_p$, $\hat{\sigma}^2_{pi}$, and $\hat{\sigma}^2_{pr:i,e}$. Weighting increased the precision of the variance components obtained in the 750-examinees-by-4-raters and 1500-examinees-by-4-rater conditions. In contrast to the weighted components, unweighted variance components manifested standard errors that were larger and more different from the theoretical standard errors, which are shown as horizontal lines in Figure 7, Figure 9, and Figure 11. The improvements in precision due to weighting, averaged across the eight conditions (2 *batch sizes* x 2 levels of the *item effect* x 2 levels of the *person-by-rater effect*), were 0.015 (4.3% of the population value), 0.010 (3.3%), and 0.003 (1%) for $\hat{\sigma}^2_p$, $\hat{\sigma}^2_{pi}$, and $\hat{\sigma}^2_{pr:i,e}$, respectively. Weighting increased the precision of composite indices $E\rho^2$ and $\phi(\lambda)$ with an average 0.019 (2.1% of the population values) and 0.013 (1.3%), respectively.

When the data subsets were very similar in size (i.e., those with expected subset size equal the minimum batch size) the differences in precision between the weighted and unweighted components were negligible. All increments in precision were less than 0.0035. These conditions included 750-examinees-by-2-raters, 750 x 8, 1500 x 8, 1500 x 14, and all other conditions with 3000 or more examinees. This finding applied to the *person* (Figure 6 and Figure 7), *person-by-item* (Figure 8 and Figure 9), and *person-by-rater-nested-within-item* (Figure 10 and Figure 11) effects. The difference in precision was too low to influence any high-stake decisions based on the composite indices.

When there was no subsampling of raters (i.e., 750-examinees-by-2-raters), weighting did not influence the precision at all (no increment in precision was present with rounding error at 7 decimal places). The data series labeled 750-examinee-by-2-rater in Figure 6, Figure 8 and Figure 10 were identical to those in their corresponding figures showing the unweighted results.

Weighting by subset size did not increase the precision in conditions where the target facets were unrelated to the object of measurement (increased precision only by 0.5% and 2.5% of the population values of $\hat{\sigma}^2_i$ and $\hat{\sigma}^2_{r:i}$, respectively.

As hypothesized, weighting had no effect on the *disconnected crossed* rating plan. Figures 10, 12, 14, and 16 show the weighted variance components for the *disconnected crossed rating plan.* The unweighted variance components (Figures 11, 13, 15, and 17) were recovered as precisely as the weighted estimates (i.e., the standard errors were identical between the weighted and the unweighted estimates of the seven variance components for all conditions). In addition, the empirical standard errors for both estimators matched the theoretical standard errors depicted as horizontal lines in the figures.

Comparison of the weighted and unweighted estimates for the *connected mixture* rating plan

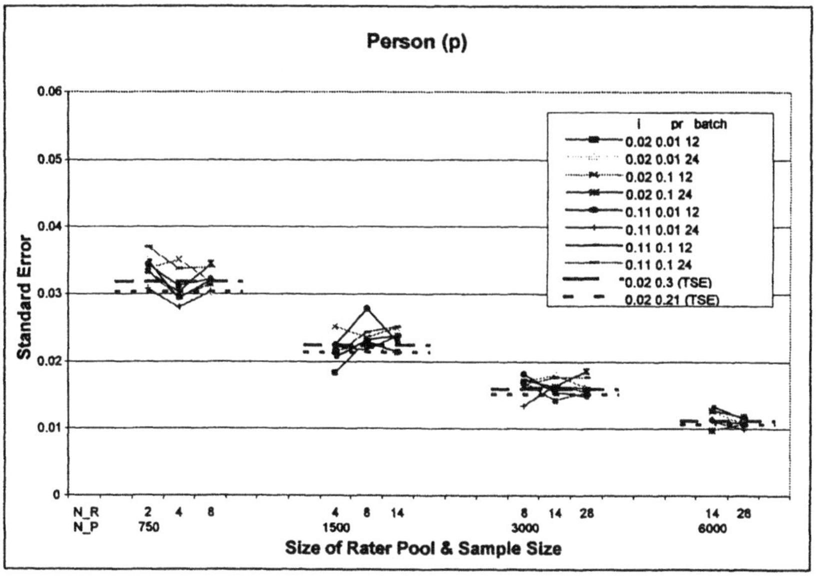

Figure 6: Weighted estimates $\hat{\sigma}_p^2$.

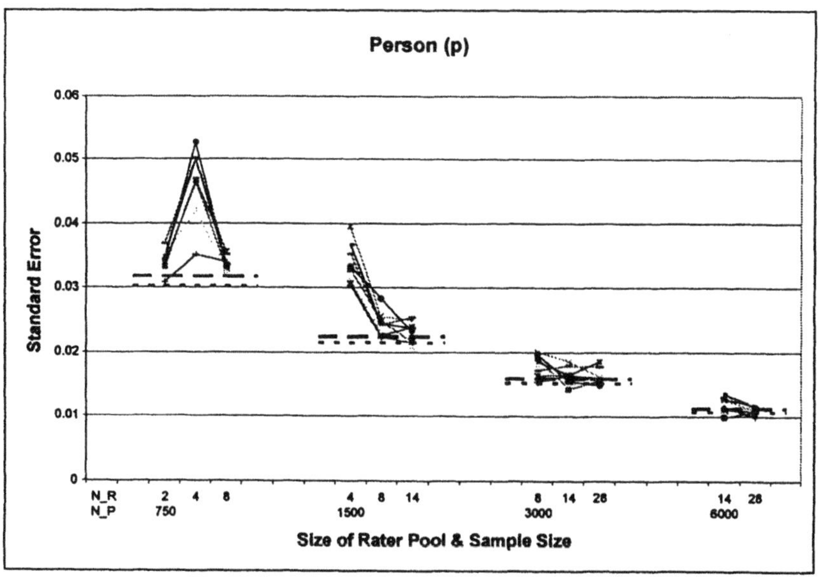

Figure 7: Unweighted estimates $\hat{\sigma}_p^2$.

Comparison of the weighted and unweighted estimates for the *connected mixture* rating plan *(continued)*

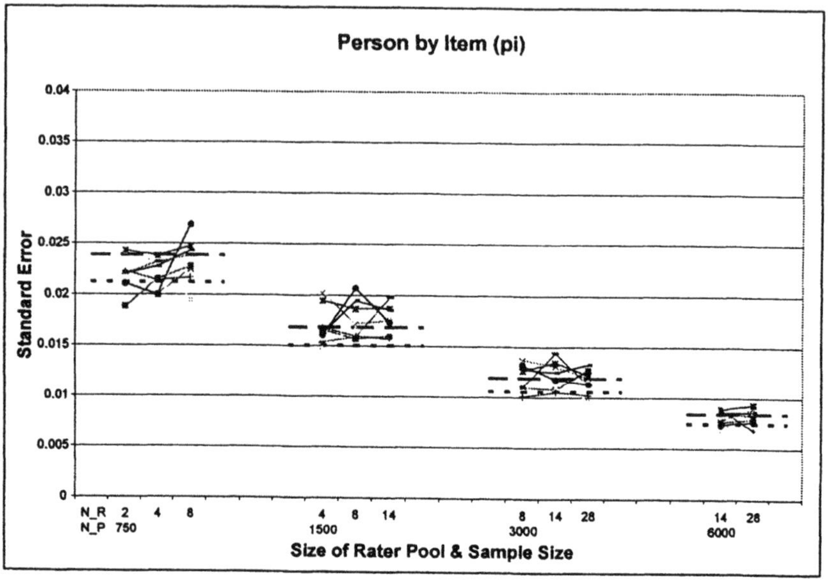

Figure 8: Weighted estimates $\hat{\sigma}^2_{pi}$.

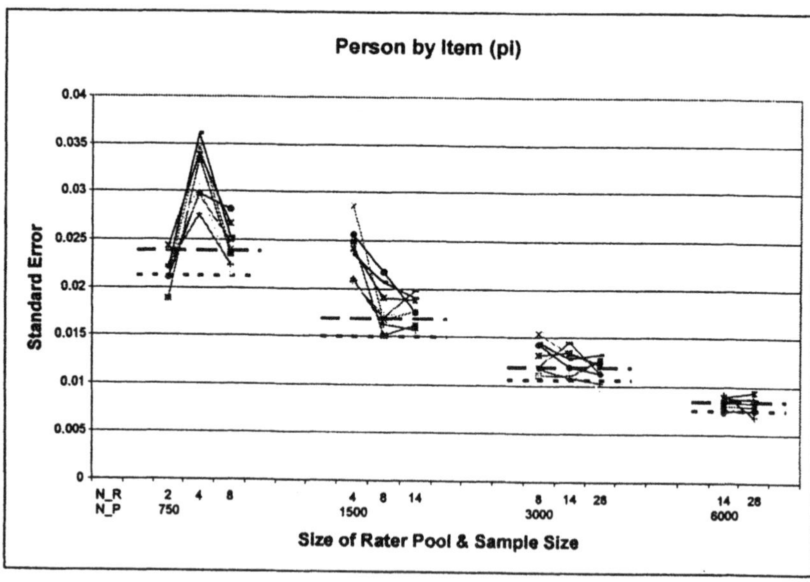

Figure 9: Unweighted estimates $\hat{\sigma}^2_{pi}$.

Comparison of the weighted and unweighted estimates for the *connected mixture* rating plan *(continued)*

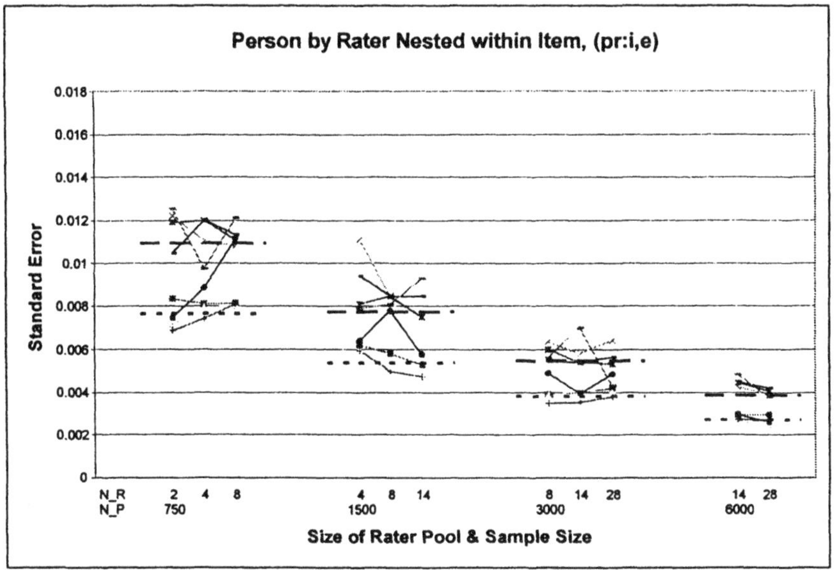

Figure 10: Weighted estimates $\hat{\sigma}^2_{pr:i,e}$.

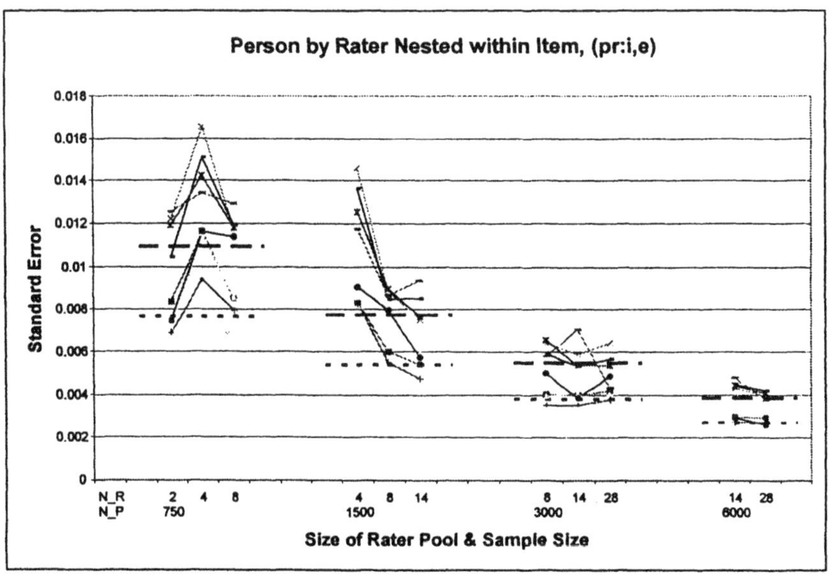

Figure 11: Unweighted estimates $\hat{\sigma}^2_{pr:i,e}$.

Comparison of the weighted and unweighted estimates for the *disconnected crossed* rating plan

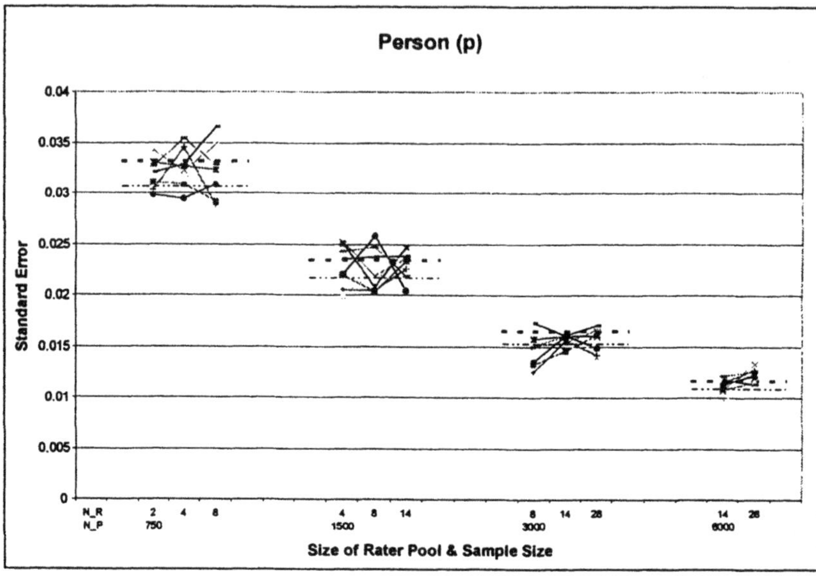

Figure 12: Weighted estimates $\hat{\sigma}_p^2$.

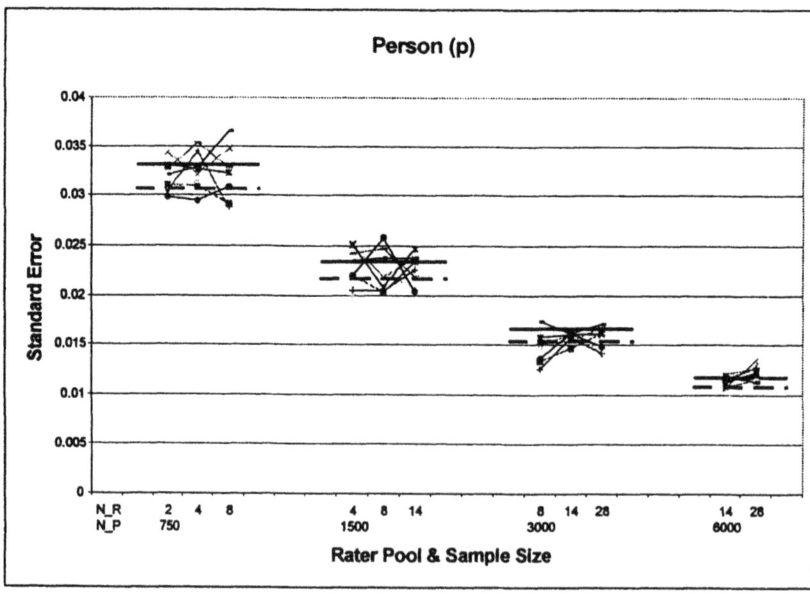

Figure 13: Unweighted estimates $\hat{\sigma}_p^2$.

Comparison of the weighted and unweighted estimates for the *disconnected crossed* rating plan *(continued)*

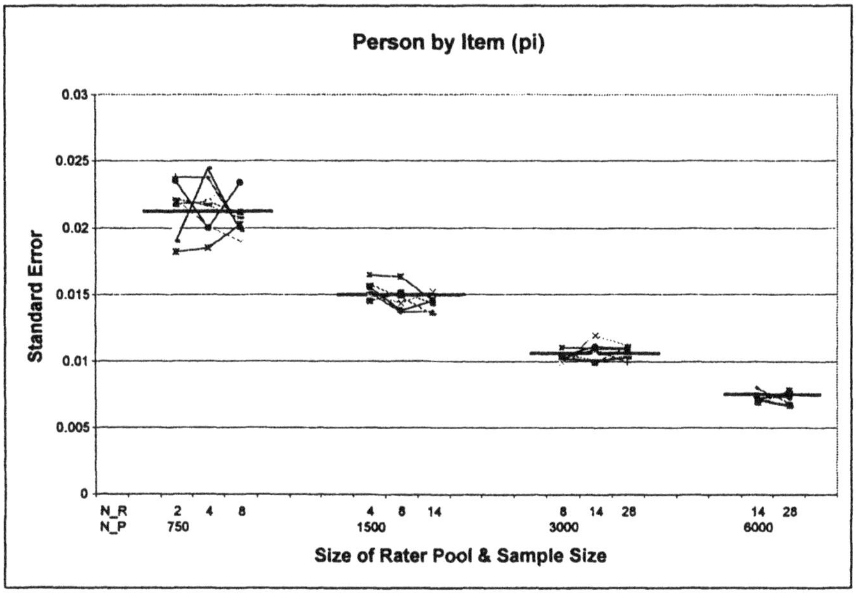

Figure 14: Weighted estimates $\hat{\sigma}^2_{pi}$.

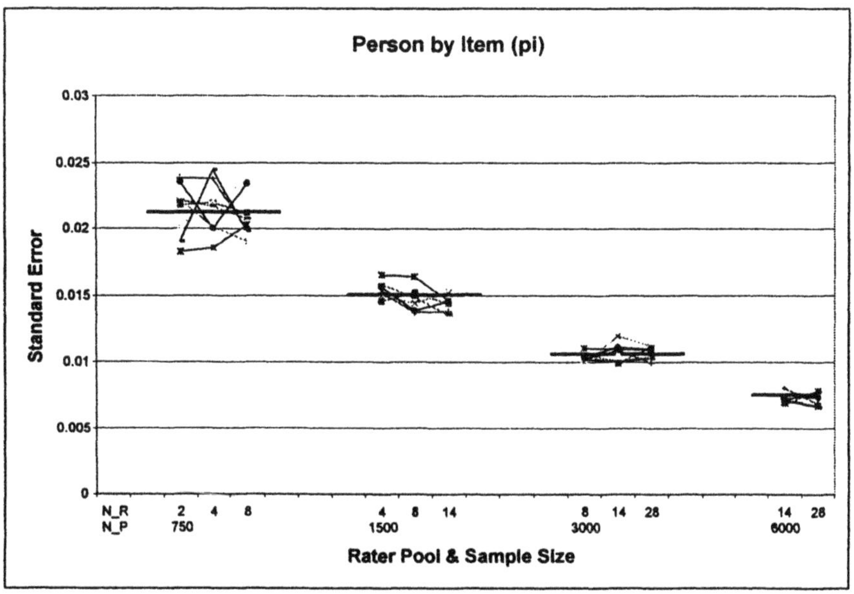

Figure 15: Unweighted estimates $\hat{\sigma}^2_{pi}$.

Comparison of the weighted and unweighted estimates for the *disconnected crossed* rating plan *(continued)*

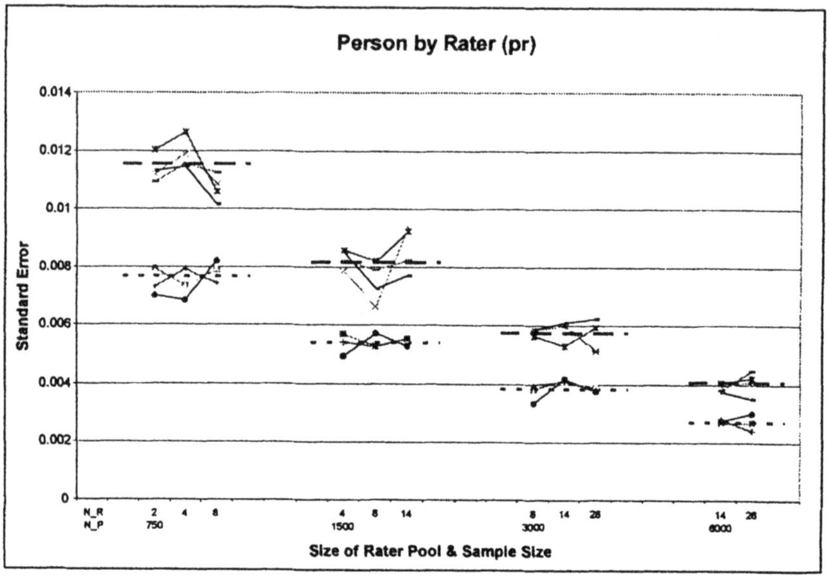

Figure 16: Weighted estimates $\hat{\sigma}^2_{pr}$.

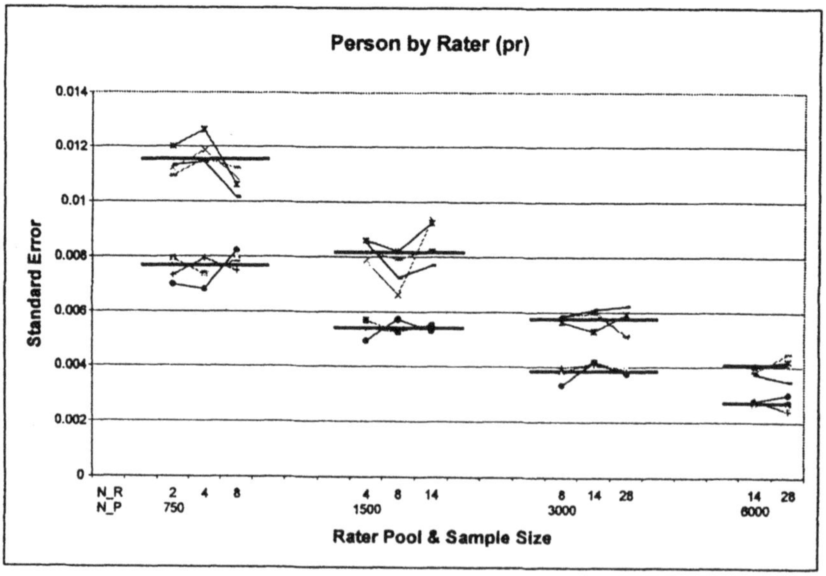

Figure 17: Unweighted estimates $\hat{\sigma}^2_{pr}$.

Comparison of the weighted and unweighted estimates for the *disconnected crossed* rating plan *(continued)*

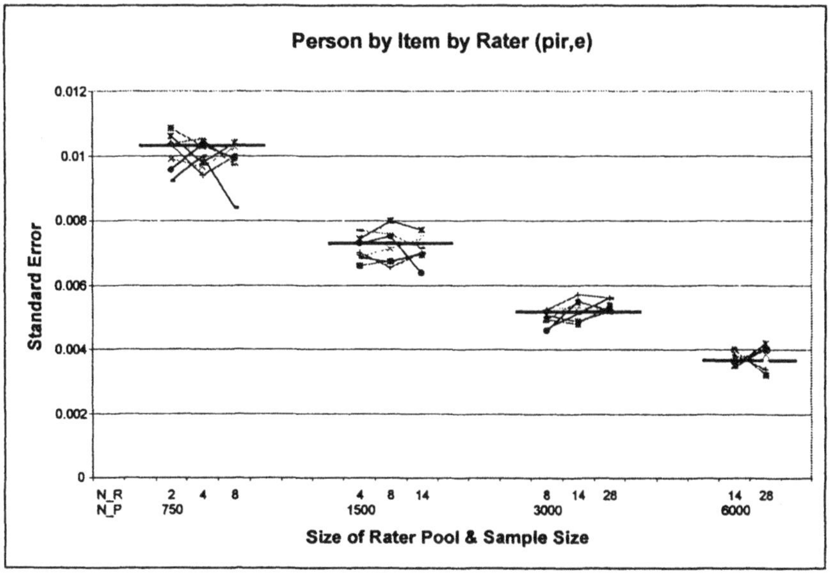

Figure 18: Weighted estimates $\hat{\sigma}^2_{pir,e}$.

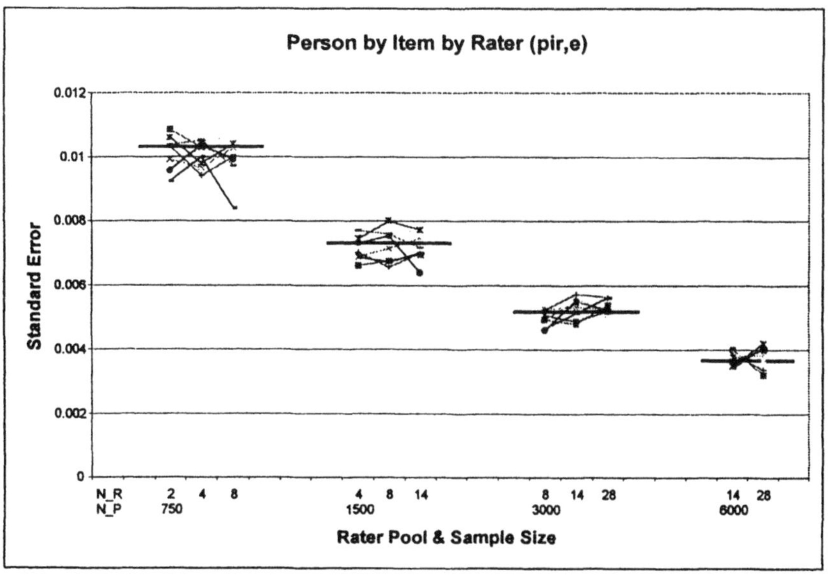

Figure 19: Unweighted estimates $\hat{\sigma}^2_{pir,e}$.

4.1.2. Accuracy

No matter whether or not variance component estimates were weighted by sample size, they were recovered with high accuracy for both the *disconnected crossed* and *connected mixture* rating plans in all 88 experimental conditions, which were composed by crossing the high and low magnitudes of σ_i^2 and σ_{pr}^2; large and small *minimum batch size*; high, medium, and low *rater pool sizes*; and the small, medium, large, very large *sample sizes*. The weighted variance component estimates differed only minimally from the unweighted estimates, in accuracy. For the *connected mixture* rating plan, the differences between the weighted and unweighted estimates of the five variance components were 0.08%, 0.34%, 0.25%, 0.10%, and 0.04%, respectively. For the *disconnected crossed* rating plan, the accuracy of the variance component estimates were close to identical; excluding the *item-by-rater* effect which had a mean difference in accuracy 0.01%, the other six variance components were identical between the weighted and unweighted conditions. Since weighting reduced the standard errors (reported in the previous section "precision") and did not lower the accuracy (reported in the current section) of variance component estimates, only the weighted estimates were examined and reported in the results that follow.

4.2. THE EFFECT OF PACKING ESSAYS INTO BATCHES OF 12 VERSUS BATCHES OF 24

Packing essays into batches of 24 as opposed to 12 did not systematically raise nor lower the accuracy and precision of variance components and composite indices in both rating plans. Table 10 on page 67 shows the range, mean, and standard deviation of the ratio between the standard errors of the variance components when using two levels of batch size (i.e., $SE(\hat{\sigma}'^2_\alpha)/SE(\hat{\sigma}^2_\alpha)$), where $\hat{\sigma}'^2_\alpha$ and $\hat{\sigma}^2_\alpha$ represent the variance components or composites obtained by using a minimum batch size of 24 and 12 respectively.

Table 10: The Ratio of *Standard Errors* of Indices Obtained Using a Batch Size of 24 to Those Obtained Using a Batch Size of 12 for the *Disconnected Crossed* Rating Plan

		Min	Mean	Max	Std	n conditions
SE Ratios for Variance Components	person	0.790	**0.996**	1.185	0.085	44
	item	0.558	**1.036**	1.639	0.272	44
	rater	0.748	**1.030**	1.660	0.176	44
	person-by-item	0.824	**1.007**	1.187	0.086	44
	person-by-rater	0.806	**1.018**	1.281	0.095	44
	item-by-rater	0.724	**1.016**	1.430	0.156	44
	person-by-item-rater, error	0.836	**1.037**	1.173	0.086	44
SE Ratios for Composite Indices	Generalizability Coefficient	0.831	**1.003**	1.240	0.096	44
	Dependability Coefficient	0.764	**1.020**	1.442	0.146	44
	Misclassification Error	0.631	**1.043**	1.603	0.247	44

Table 10 shows that the mean ratios of the standard errors across the 44 conditions for each of the variance components were very close to one (± 0.05). This result indicated that the average estimates obtained by packing essays into batches of 24 were as precise as those obtained by packing essays into batches of 12. The range of ratios was from 0.56 to 1.66. Table 11 on page 70 shows the descriptive information for the ratio of the accuracy between the two levels of batch size.

Table 11: The Ratio of *Accuracy* of Indices Obtained Using a Batch Size of 24 to Those Obtained Using a Batch Size of 12 for the *Disconnected Crossed* Rating Plan

		Min	**Mean**	Max	Std	n conditions
Accuracy Ratios for Variance Components	person	0.981	**0.998**	1.032	0.009	44
	item	0.693	**1.053**	1.569	0.224	44
	rater	0.692	**1.021**	1.432	0.171	44
	person-by-item	0.985	**1.001**	1.024	0.007	44
	person-by-rater	0.866	**1.006**	1.168	0.055	44
	item-by-rater	0.849	**1.007**	1.219	0.091	44
	person-by-item-rater, error	0.988	**0.999**	1.010	0.005	44
Accuracy Ratios for Composite Indices	Generalizability Coefficient	0.990	**0.999**	1.016	0.005	44
	Dependability Coefficient	0.978	**0.998**	1.023	0.010	44
	Misclassification Error	0.886	**1.007**	1.119	0.053	44

The results for accuracy were similar to those for precision for all the variance component estimates and the corresponding composite indices, providing no evidence that $ACCURACY(\hat{\sigma}'^2_\alpha) > ACCURACY(\hat{\sigma}^2_\alpha)$ for the *disconnected crossed* rating plan. Batch size also did not make a difference for the *connected mixture* rating plan.

Table 12 and Table 13 give the ratios of the standard error and accuracy for this rating plan.

Table 12: The Ratio of *Standard Errors* of Indices Obtained Using a Batch Size of 24 to Those Obtained Using a Batch Size of 12 for the *Connected Mixture* Rating Plan

		Min	Mean	Max	Std
SE Ratios for Variance Components	person	0.733	**0.997**	1.157	0.090
	item	0.570	**1.009**	1.767	0.293
	rater	0.757	**1.019**	1.358	0.122
	person-by-item	0.763	**0.995**	1.281	0.124
	person-by-rater-nested-in-item, error	0.638	**0.947**	1.299	0.138
SE Ratios for Composite Indices	Generalizability Coefficient	0.727	**1.012**	1.244	0.111
	Dependability Coefficient	0.727	**1.012**	1.244	0.111
	Misclassification Error	0.575	**1.017**	1.727	0.272

Table 13: The Ratio of *Accuracy* of Indices Obtained Using a Batch Size of 24 to Those Obtained Using a Batch Size of 12 for the *Connected Mixture* Rating Plan

		Min	Mean	Max	Std
Accuracy Ratio for Variance Components	person	0.968	**1.002**	1.024	0.010
	item	0.608	**1.045**	1.793	0.285
	rater-nested-in-item	0.863	**1.016**	1.230	0.082
	person-by-item	0.989	**1.001**	1.027	0.007
	person-by-item-by-rater, error	0.992	**1.000**	1.015	0.005
Accuracy Ratio for Composite Indices	Generalizability Coefficient	0.982	**1.000**	1.011	0.005
	Dependability Coefficient	0.971	**1.000**	1.039	0.014
	Misclassification Error	0.781	**1.008**	1.266	0.090

4.3. ACCURACY OF THE VARIANCE COMPONENTS FOR TWO RATING PLANS

The mean accuracy of the variance component estimates in the two rating plans was high. For the *disconnected crossed* rating plan, the mean accuracy across the 88 conditions was 100% ± 0.8%. The mean accuracy for reliably scoring a measurement procedure to make norm-referenced decisions (using the generalizability coefficient) was 99.8% and the mean accuracy for making criterion-referenced decisions (using the dependability coefficient) was 100.5% (see Table 14). For the *connected mixture* rating plan, the mean accuracy of recovering the five variance component estimates, shown in Table 15, was 100% ± 0.5%. In addition, the mean accuracy of the generalizability and dependability coefficients were 99.9% and 100.6%, respectively.

Table 14: Accuracy of the *Disconnected Crossed* Rating Plan

		Min	Mean	Max	Std	n conditions
Accuracy of the Variance Components	person	0.982	0.999	1.026	0.006	88
	item	0.685	0.992	1.251	0.142	88
	rater	0.682	0.993	1.291	0.126	88
	person-by-item	0.986	1.002	1.013	0.005	88
	person-by-rater	0.874	1.002	1.119	0.040	88
	item-by-rater	0.811	1.008	1.431	0.079	88
	person-by-item-rater, error	0.991	1.001	1.011	0.004	88
						88
Accuracy of Composite Indices	Generalizability Coefficient	0.989	0.998	1.005	0.003	88
	Dependability Coefficient	0.957	1.005	1.049	0.011	88
	Misclassification Error	0.901	1.005	1.110	0.037	88

Table 15: Accuracy of the *Connected Mixture* Rating Plan

		Min	Mean	Max	Std	n conditions
Accuracy of Variance Components	person	0.984	1.001	1.017	0.006	88
	item	0.679	1.005	1.374	0.169	88
	rater: item	0.825	0.995	1.098	0.053	88
	person-by-item	0.987	1.001	1.014	0.005	88
	person-by-rater-nested-within-item, error	0.993	1.001	1.009	0.003	88
Accuracy of Composite Indices	Generalizability Coefficient	0.989	0.999	1.008	0.003	88
	Dependability Coefficient	0.986	1.006	1.031	0.011	88
	Misclassification Error	0.869	1.010	1.204	0.055	88

For the accuracy of variance components reported in Tables 14 and 15, the accuracy of the *person* and *person-by-item* effects were very similar between the two rating plans, in terms of minimum, mean, maximum, and standard deviations. Although the accuracy of the *item* effects in both rating plans had the largest standard deviations among all other effects, the means of these two accuracy indices tended to converge to one (i.e., 100% accuracy). Such convergence suggested that 100 replications was insufficient to assess the accuracy (or unbiasedness) of the *item* effect. Collapsing across the 88 conditions, however, increased the number of replications to 88,000 and thus provided ample replications to evaluate the highly variable *item* effect, which appeared to be accurately estimated by the subdividing method. Tables 14 and 15 show that the mean accuracy for *item* effects were, respectively, 99.2% and 100.5% for the *disconnected crossed* and *connected mixture* rating plans.

4.4. PRECISION OF THE SUBDIVIDING METHOD AND THE EFFECTS OF EXPANDING RATER POOL SIZES

In this section, I investigated the degree to which the expansion of rater pool sizes influenced the precision of the facets that are related to the rater effects, namely the *rater*, *item-by-*rater, and *person-by-rater* effect. The *rater* main effect is examined first, followed by the *item-by-rater* interaction effect. The *person-by-rater* interaction effect, which was hypothesized to be influenced the least by the rater pool size, is discussed last.

Figure 20 summarizes the values of $SE(\hat{\sigma}_r^2)$, corresponding to the *disconnected crossed* rating plan for all the levels of *sample size, rater pool, minimum batch size, item effect,* and *person-by-rater effect.* The precision of the *rater* effect varied only minimally among the different levels of *item* effect, *person-by-rater* effect, and *batch size*. The major variation due to the size of rater pool; the $SE(\hat{\sigma}_r^2)$ decreased considerably as the *rater pool* expanded, holding the sample size constant. The percent decrease in standard error was lower than one half of the percent increase in the rater pool size. The two horizontal lines, for high and low *person-by-rater* effect conditions ($\sigma_{pr}^2 = 0.1$ and 0.01), representing the theoretical standard errors for σ_r^2 coincide at 0.0131. Even though the theoretical and empirical standard errors were supposed to be the same or at least very close in the conditions where there was no missing data (i.e., 2-rater-750-examinee conditions), the empirical standard errors appeared to be larger than the theoretical standard errors. This finding was not surprising. Rather, it reflected the inaccuracy of the theoretical standard errors based on a small number of levels in a facet. Chapter 5 on provides a thorough discussion.

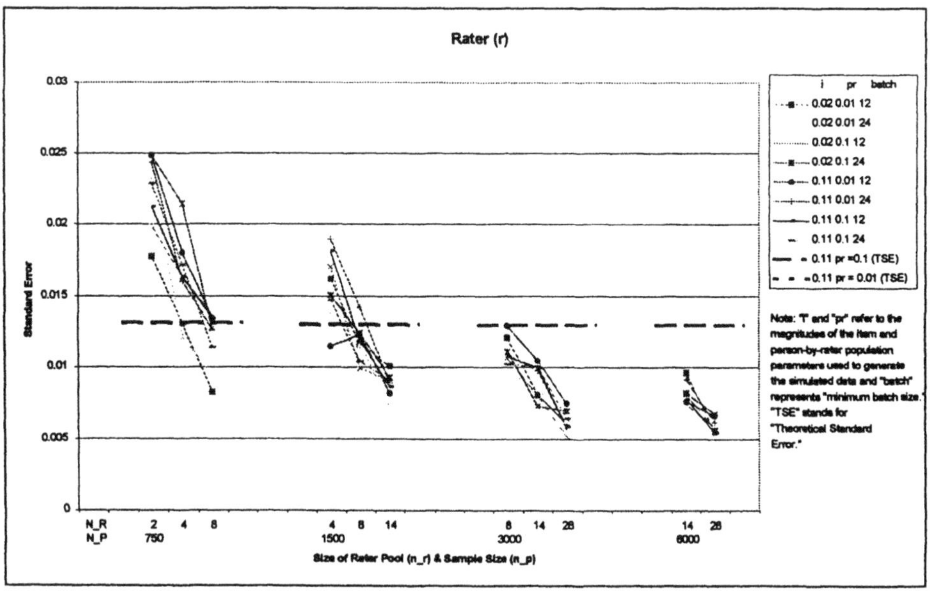

Figure 20: The reduction of standard error for the rater effect as a function of the size of rater pool and sample size.

Table 16 displays the average SEs and average reductions of standard error in percentage terms. As the rater pool size increased from 2 to 4 (a 100% increase), the standard error declined from 0.0224 to 0.0163 with a 27% reduction, averaged across *item effect, person-by-rater effect, and minimum batch size.* While holding the rater pool size constant at any value, increases in sample size did not lead to sizeable decreases in standard error. For instance, given a pool of eight raters, the range of $SE(\hat{\sigma}_r^2)$ was 0.0115 ± 0.0005, despite sample size increases from 750, to 1500, and to 3000.

Given that the standard error of the *rater* effect was 0.0060 when one assigned random pairs of raters from a pool of 28 to score 6,000 examinees, how large should the rater pool be if one wanted to maintain the standard error by assigning ALL raters to score the examinees? Approximately a pool of 13 raters is needed. The parenthesized numbers in Table 16 show this projection and projections for a variety of rater pool sizes for 750, 1500, 3000, and 6000 examinees.

Table 16: Average SEs and Average Reduction in Empirical Standard Error for the Rater Effect

$\sigma(\hat{\sigma}^2_r)$	Size of Rater Pool				
Sample Size	2	4	8	14	28
		27%	27%		
750	0.0224 (2)	0.0163 (2)	0.0119 (2)		
			25%	25%	
1500		0.0157 (2)	0.0117 (2)	0.0088 (5)	
				18%	31%
3000			0.0110 (3)	0.0090 (5)	0.0062 (12)
					27%
6000				0.0083 (6)	0.0060 (13)

The numbers in parentheses refer to the number of raters needed to maintain an equivalent level of standard error when all raters in the rater pool score a task. The standard errors reported are averaged across *batch size, item* effect, *and person-by-rater effect.* Equation (36) in Appendix B was used to obtain the projections shown in parentheses. The standard error to the left of the parenthesized numbers were substituted into the left hand size of Equation (36). The Generalized Reduced Gradient (GRG2) nonlinear optimization method (developed by Leon Lasdon, University of Texas at Austin, and Allan Waren, Cleveland State University) in the Microsoft Excel Solver 1995 was used to solve the equation for the size of rater pool (n_r).

Figure 21 shows standard errors of the *item-by-rater* effect. The trends in the SEs resemble those for the *rater* effect, indicating that expanding the size of a rater pool reduced the standard error of the *item-by-rater* effect.

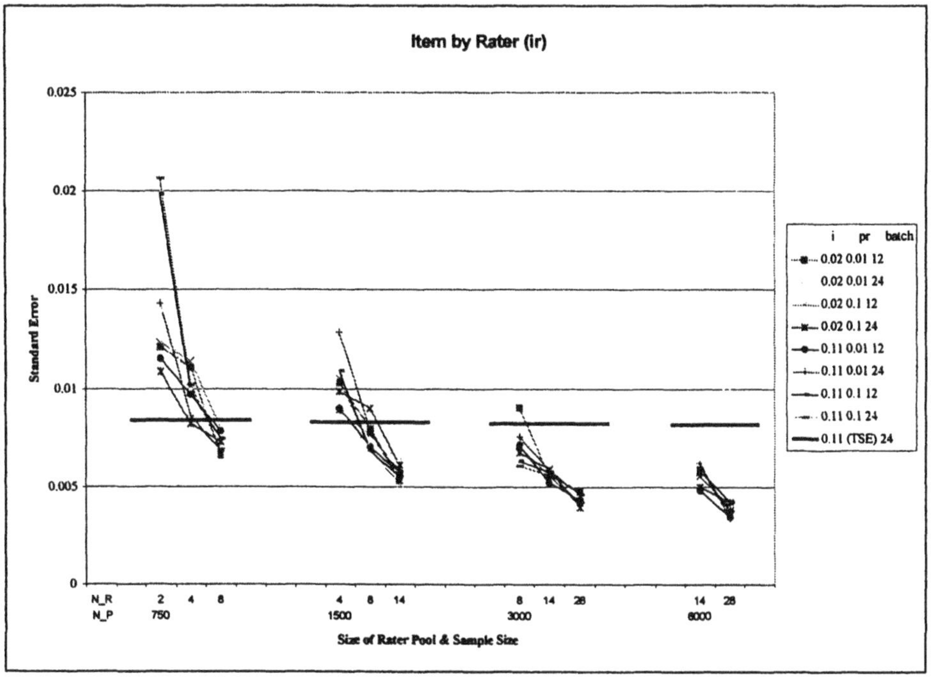

Figure 21: The reduction trends of the standard error of the rater-by-item effect.

Table 17 shows that the percent reduction in standard error was less than one half of the percent increase in the size of rater pool for the *item-by-rater* effect. The standard error obtained by subsampling from 28 raters can be obtained by employing five raters without sampling. This projection was also reported for sampling from 14, 8, 4, and 2 raters, respectively.

Table 17: Relationship Between Size of Rater Pool and Reduction in Standard Error of the Item-By-Rater Effect as a Function of Sample Size

$\sigma(\hat{\sigma}^2_{ir})$	Size of Rater Pool				
Sample Size	2	4	8	14	28
	32%		25%		
750	0.0145 (2)	0.0099 (2)	0.0074 (2)		
		24%		25%	
1500		0.0100 (2)	0.0076 (2)	0.0057 (3)	
			20%		24%
3000			0.0072 (2)	0.0058 (3)	0.0044 (5)
				29%	
6000				0.0055 (3)	0.0039 (5)

Note: The numbers in parathenses refer to the number of raters needed to maintain an equivalent level of standard error when all raters in the rater pool score a task.

Figure 22 shows values of the standard error of the *person-by-rater* effect. The standard error decreased as the sample size increased, holding constant the size of the rater pool. Expanding the rater pool did not increase precision for the *person-by-rater* effect. The two series of trends clustered around the two reference lines for the two levels of theoretical standard errors, indicating that the $SE(\hat{\sigma}^2_{pr})$ obtained by subsampling was comparable to that obtained by employing two raters regardless of the size of the rater pool.

Table 18 shows the percent reduction in the SEs as a function of the sample size given a small *person-by-rater* effect (σ^2_{pr} =0.01). The percentages of standard error reduction for all the conditions were less than the percent of increase in sample size and all increments to sample size reduce the standard errors. This observation also applied for a large *person-by-rater* effect (σ^2_{pr} =0.10).

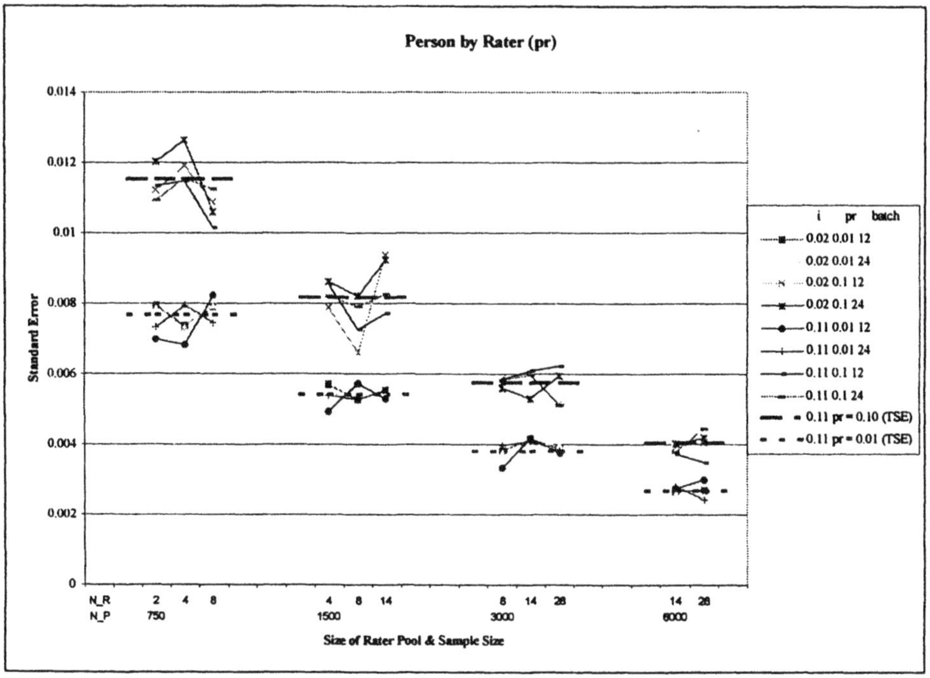

Figure 22: The standard error of the *person-by-rater* effect as a function of sample size.

Table 18: SE and Changes in Standard Error of the *Person-By-Rater* Effect as Sample Size Increases

$\sigma(\hat{\sigma}^2_{pr})$		Size of Rater Pool: 2	4	8	14	28
Sample Size	750	0.0075	0.0074	0.0079		
	1500		27% 0.0053	30% 0.0055	0.0055	
	3000			32% 0.0037	25% 0.0041	0.0039
	6000				34% 0.0027	31% 0.0027

4.5. PRECISION OF THE SUBDIVIDING METHOD AND THE EFFECTS OF INCREASING VOLUME OF EXAMINEES

Figure 23 and Figure 24 show the standard error of the object of measurement $\hat{\sigma}_p^2$ and the person-by-item-by-rater (plus systematic and non-systematic errors) effect $\hat{\sigma}_{pir,e}^2$ as a function of sample size, rater pool size, and three other simulation parameters. For $\hat{\sigma}_p^2$, the two horizontal reference lines represent the theoretical standard errors, given two raters. The top and bottom reference lines reflect standard errors for a large and a small person-by-rater effect. The empirical standard errors clustered closely around the two theoretical referenced lines and the standard errors exhibited a pattern similar to that was found for the person-by-rater effect. The values of $SE(\hat{\sigma}_p^2)$ reduced by less than 50% as the sample size doubled. Expanding the size of rater pool had inconsistent, thus ignorable effects on $SE(\hat{\sigma}_p^2)$. The standard errors of $\hat{\sigma}_{pir,e}^2$ resembled those of $\hat{\sigma}_p^2$ -- increase in the rater pool size had a marginal effect on the reduction of standard error whereas increase in sample size had a significant effect.

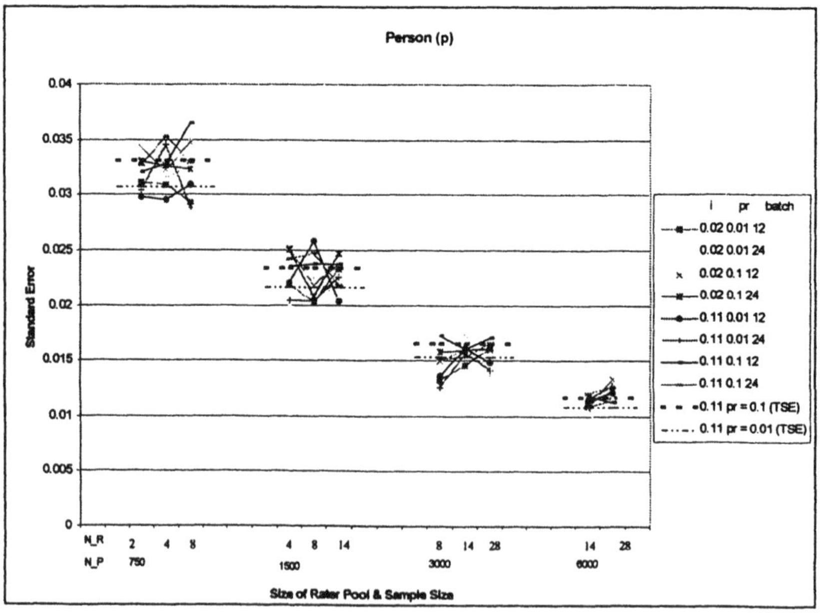

Figure 23: The standard error of the person effect as a function of sample size and rater pool size.

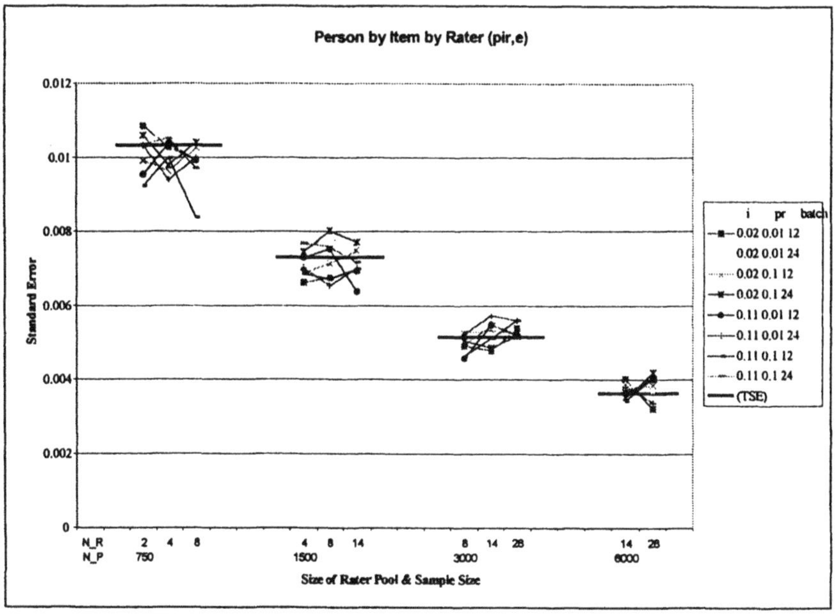

Figure 24: The standard error of the person-by-item-by-rater effect as a function of sample size and rater pool size.

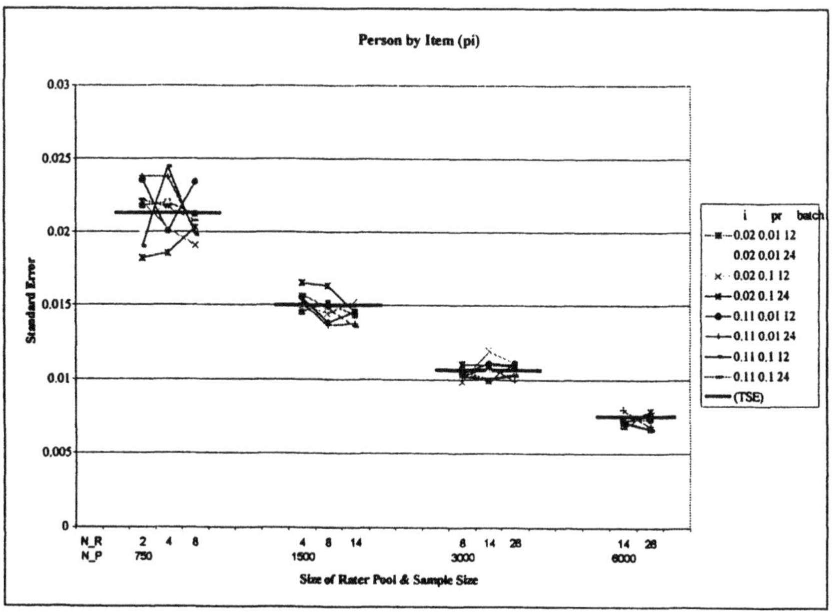

Figure 25: The standard error of the person-by-item effect as a function of sample size.

Figure 25 depicted the standard errors of the *person-by-item* effect and it shows results coherent with those for the previous three variance components $\hat{\sigma}^2_p$, $\hat{\sigma}^2_{pr}$, and $\hat{\sigma}^2_{pir,e}$. Specifically, the statistical property of consistency (the larger the sample size the smaller the variability) holds true for the subdividing method for the *disconnected crossed* rating plan.

4.6. FINDINGS ON THE DISCONNECTED CROSSED AND THE CONNECTED MIXTURE RATING PLANS

The complexity of the *connected mixture* rating plan causes scores to be allocated unevenly to the three structural designs (*crossed*, *MBIB*, and *nested*). As predicted by the decision rules discussed on page 32, the percentage of *crossed* and *MBIB* data subsets (e.g., percentage of the *crossed* data subsets = Equation (9) / Equation (12) *100%) diminished as the size of rater pool expanded. Because fewer data points were allocated for these two structural designs, the *person-by-rater* effect was less precise for a larger rater pool than it was given a smaller pool of raters. Table 19 summarizes that the expansion of the rater pool decreased the certainty of the *person-by-rater* effect.

Table 19: Increases in Uncertainty of the *Person-By-Rater* Effect in the *Connected Mixture* Rating Plan

$\sigma(\hat{\sigma}^2_{pr})$	4	8	14	28
(rater pool increase)		100%	75%	100%
Sample Size		49%		
750	0.0226	0.0338		
		54%	21%	
1500	0.0162	0.0249	0.0302	
			31%	47%
3000		0.0168	0.0219	0.0323
				44%
6000			0.0160	0.0230

It can be observed that all the increase in imprecision (or increase in SEs) in Table 19 (indicated by arrows) were less than approximately five percent in addition to half of the percentage increase in the rater pool size. Expanding the rater pool size from four to eight raters yielded a 100% increase in rater pool size and the increases in uncertainty for the *person-by-rater* effect were 49% and 54%, respectively, for sample sizes 750 and 1500. The corresponding increases in uncertainty became lower (21% and 31% for sample sizes 1,500 and 3,000) as the rater pool expanded by a lower percentage, 75% as opposed to 100% (from eight to 14 raters). The increases in uncertainty returned to the mid- and high- forty percent (47% and 44%) when the rater pool expanded by 100%, for sample sizes 3,000 and 6,000. All of the above reductions were less than 55% (0.5 * 100% + 5%).

Figure 26 depicts the phenomenon reported in Table 19 accompanied by the theoretical standard errors. These theoretical standard errors predicted the *person-by-rater* effect based on the same two raters scoring all the examinees on all items (i.e., completely balanced situations with a crossed structural design).

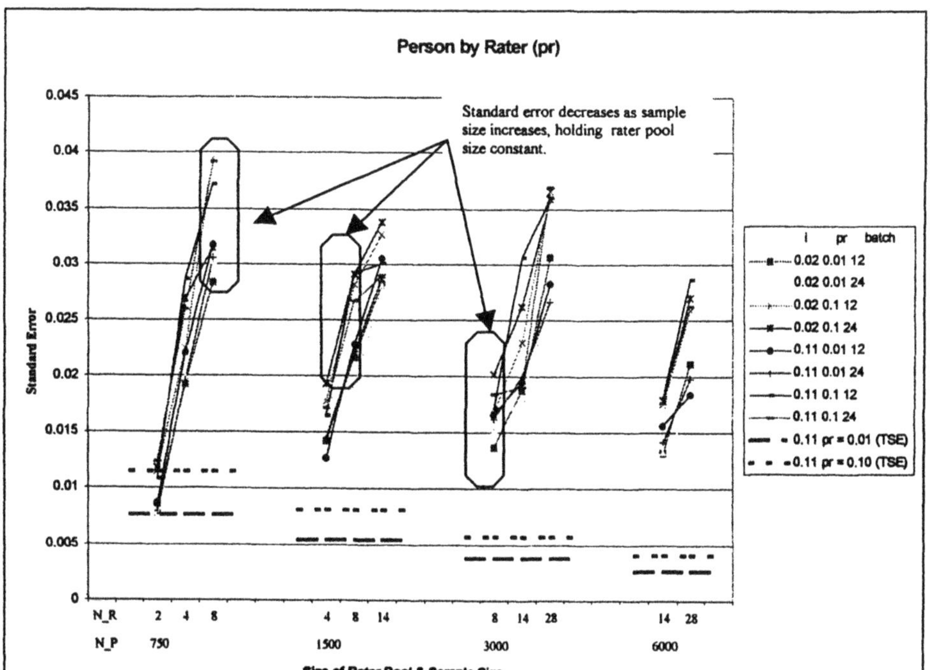

Figure 26: The relationship between the improvement of the person-by-rater effect and the expansion of sample size using the *connected mixture* rating plan.

As observed in the above figure, the larger the rater pool, the farther was the empirical standard error from the theoretical standard error. This indicates that one would become less confident of the *person-by-rater* effect as more raters were employed, holding the number of examinees constant.

The increase in sample size had an opposite effect than that of expanding the size of rater pool — holding the size of rater pool constant, the larger the sample size, the higher the precision (and the smaller the SEs). Such observations applied to all four levels of sample size. The trend shows the increase in precision as the sample size increased from 750, 1500, to 3000, holding constant the size of rater pool (the three boxes in Figure 26 on page 83 highlight the 8-rater pool examples; the larger the sample size, the smaller the SEs). The means of $SE(\hat{\sigma}^2_{pr})$ were 0.0315, 0.0249, and 0.0144 for the three levels of sample sizes (750, 1500, and 3000). The minimum reduction in $SE(\hat{\sigma}^2_{pr})$, from one level of sample size to another, was over 25%.

Figure 27 compares the degree of uncertainty of the *person-by-rater* effect in the *connected mixture* rating plan to that in the *disconnected crossed* rating plan ($SE(\hat{\sigma}^2_{pr})-SE(\hat{\sigma}^2_{pr'})$), where $\hat{\sigma}^2_{pr}$ and $\hat{\sigma}^2_{pr'}$ represented the *person-by-rater* effects in the *disconnected crossed* and *connected mixture* rating plans, respectively. The $\hat{\sigma}^2_{pr}$ was estimated with a higher degree of precision in the *disconnected crossed* rating plan. On average across all the conditions for the 750-examinee conditions, $\hat{\sigma}^2_{pr}$ was estimated with a precision 0.0127 higher than it was estimated in the *connected mixture* rating plan. For the 1500-, 3000-, and 6000- examinee conditions, $\hat{\sigma}^2_{pr}$ was estimated with even higher precision: mean differences were 0.0170, 0.0189, and 0.0161, respectively.

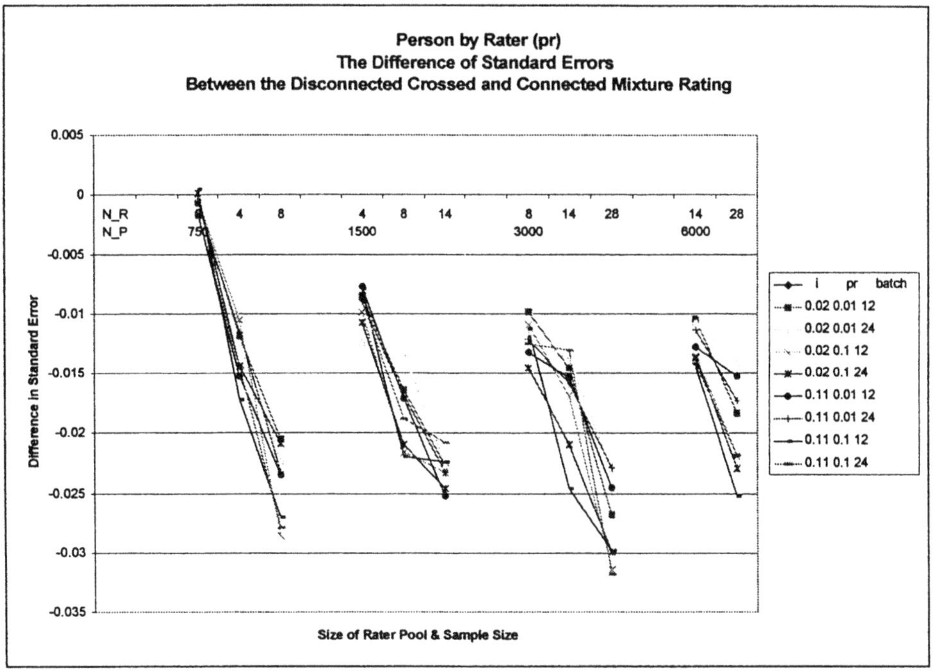

Figure 27: The effect of employing two different rating plans on the precision of the person-by-rater effect.

As was true for $\hat{\sigma}^2_{pr}$, five other variance components (all except the *item* effect) manifested increasing imprecision as the size of rater pool expanded in the *connected mixture* rating plan. This is likely due to the reduction of data (discussed in the Methodology section) falling into the *crossed* and *MBIB* designs. Figure 28 displays this effect for $SE(\hat{\sigma}^2_{pir,e})$.

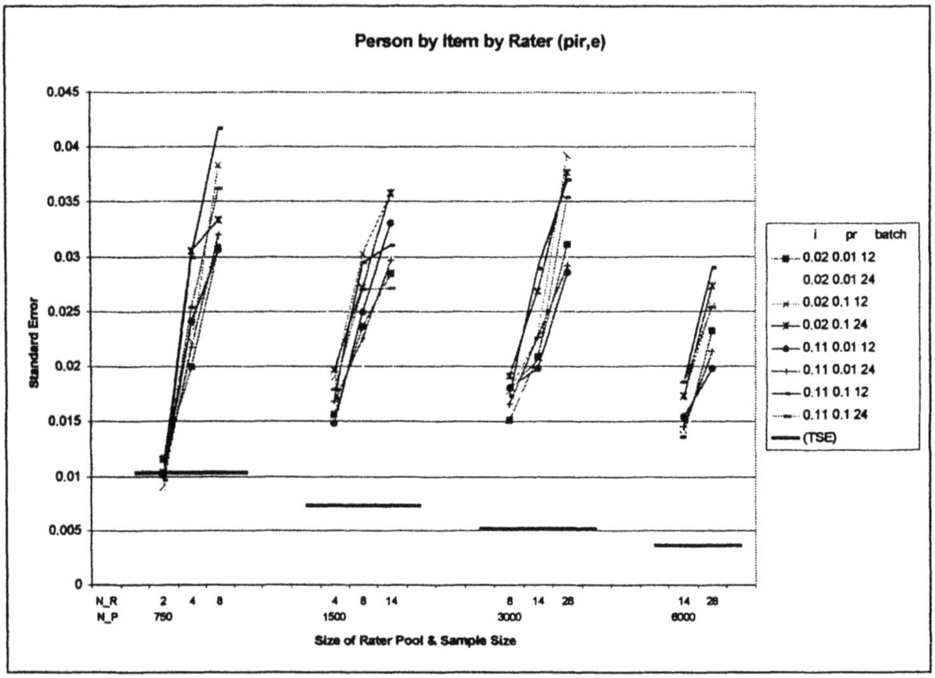

Figure 28: The relationship between the improvement of the person-by-item-by-rater effect and the expansion of the rater pool size using the *connected mixture* rating plan.

In order to utilize all the available data in the *connected mixture* rating plan, four of the seven variance components obtained in the previous section were summed to parallel the five variance components in the *nested* design, namely $\hat{\sigma}^2_{r:i} = \hat{\sigma}^2_r + \hat{\sigma}^2_{ir}$ and $\hat{\sigma}^2_{pr:i,e} = \hat{\sigma}^2_{pr} + \hat{\sigma}^2_{pir,e}$. Figure 29 presents the precision of $\hat{\sigma}^2_{r:i}$ obtained by the reconfiguration. The $\hat{\sigma}^2_{r:i}$ became more stable as the rater pool expanded indicating that recruiting more raters while using only a random pair to score an examinee can add to precision in estimating either one or both of the following two measurement errors — (1) variability due to rater scoring examinees differently, averaged across items, namely $\hat{\sigma}^2_r$; and (2) variability due to rater scoring items *differentially* different averaged across examinees, namely $\hat{\sigma}^2_{ir}$.

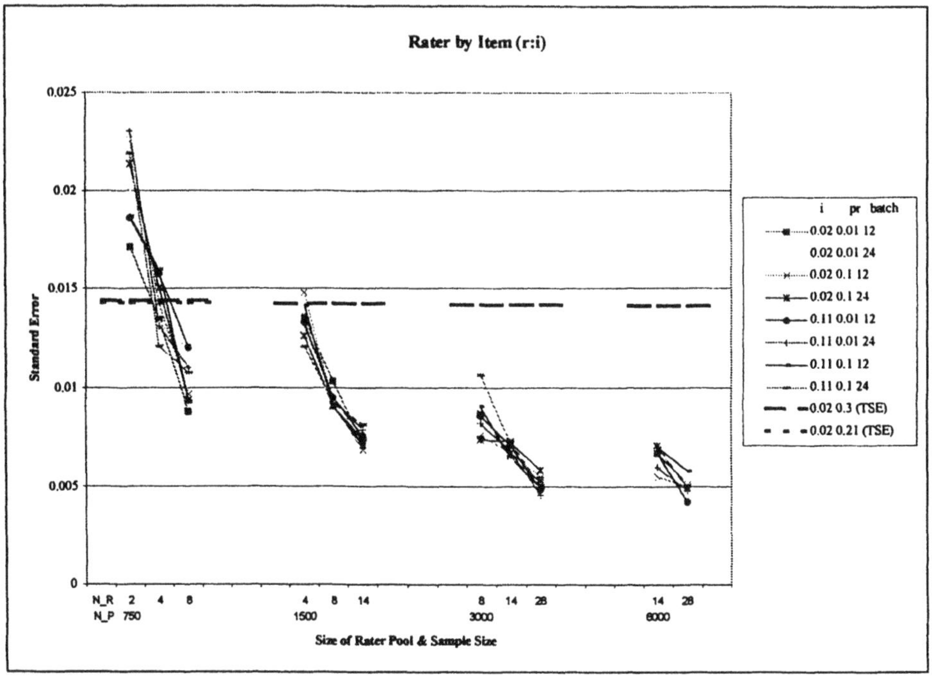

Figure 29: The decrease in standard error as a function of rater pool size after utilizing all the available data.

The average standard error for the 750-examinees conditions (averaged across the *item* effect, *person-by-item* effect, and *batch size*) decreased from 0.0205 to 0.0141, and went further down to 0.0103 yielding a reduction trend of 31% and 27%. The average standard error for the 1500-examinee conditions showed a similar reduction rate with a 30% (0.0135 to 0.0093) decline from sampling 2 of 4 raters to sampling 2 of 8 raters and with a 20% reduction from the 8-rater conditions to the 14-rater conditions. For the 3000-examinee conditions, the decreases were 26% (0.0086 to 0.0068) and 25% (0.0068 to 0.0051), respectively, for the 8-to14-rater expansion and the 14-to-28-rater expansion. Increasing from a pool of 14 raters to 28 raters reduced the average standard error by 23% (0.0065 to 0.005) for a sample of 6000 examinees.

4.7. PRECISION OF THE SUBDIVIDING METHOD FOR ITEM EFFECTS

4.7.1 Disconnected Crossed Rating Plan

Figure 30 shows that there is no relationship between the *sample size*, *rater pool size* and the standard error for the item effect, as hypothesized in research question 4 (see section 3.4.1). This finding was expected because adding more raters or increasing the volume of examinees should have very little influence in determining the certainty of the variations in item difficulty. The standard errors fluctuated slightly above the reference lines (for the two item-effect parameter values), indicating that the simulated variance components were more variable than were suggested by theory for two raters (Again note that the theoretical values do not account for sampling from a rater pool).

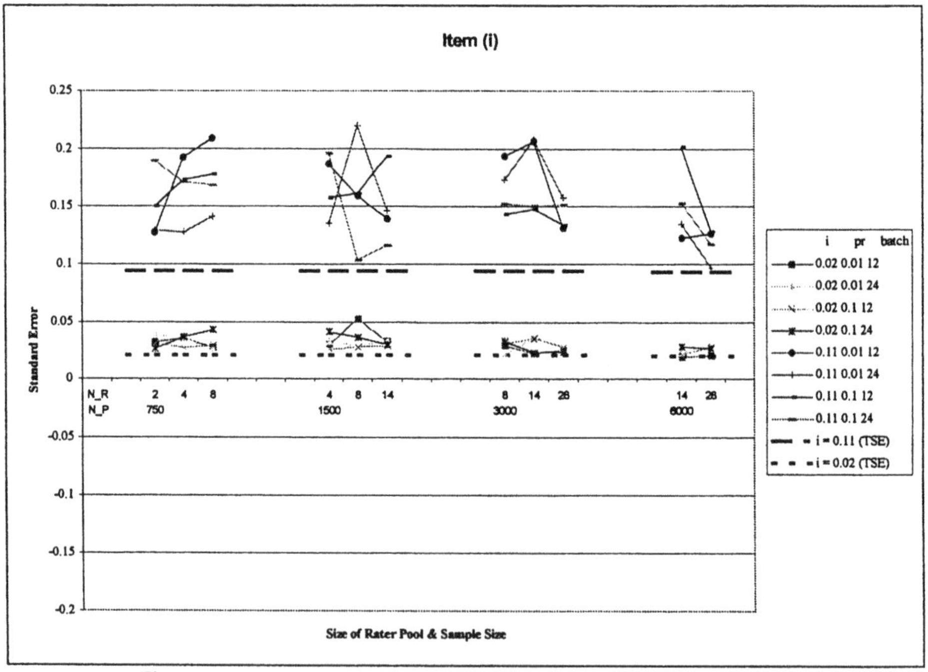

Figure 30: The randomness of the standard errors for the item effect (*disconnected crossed* rating plan).

4.7.2. Connected Mixture Rating Plan

Figure 31 depicts the precision of $\hat{\sigma}_i^2$ which was not influenced by the size of rater pool and sample size. The series of $\hat{\sigma}_i^2$ which were generated with a population value 0.02 were recovered with a smaller degree of variation than those generated with a population value 0.11. As expected, the two series were separated distinctly in Figure 31 with the larger-variability series associated with larger and a more conservative standard error than suggested by theory. The average empirical standard error was 0.159 comparing to the theoretical standard error 0.098 based on two raters. This difference was expected (Brennan, 1992) because the theoretical standard error relied on asymptotic assumptions, which were not viable when the number of levels in the *item* facet was small (i.e., 2).

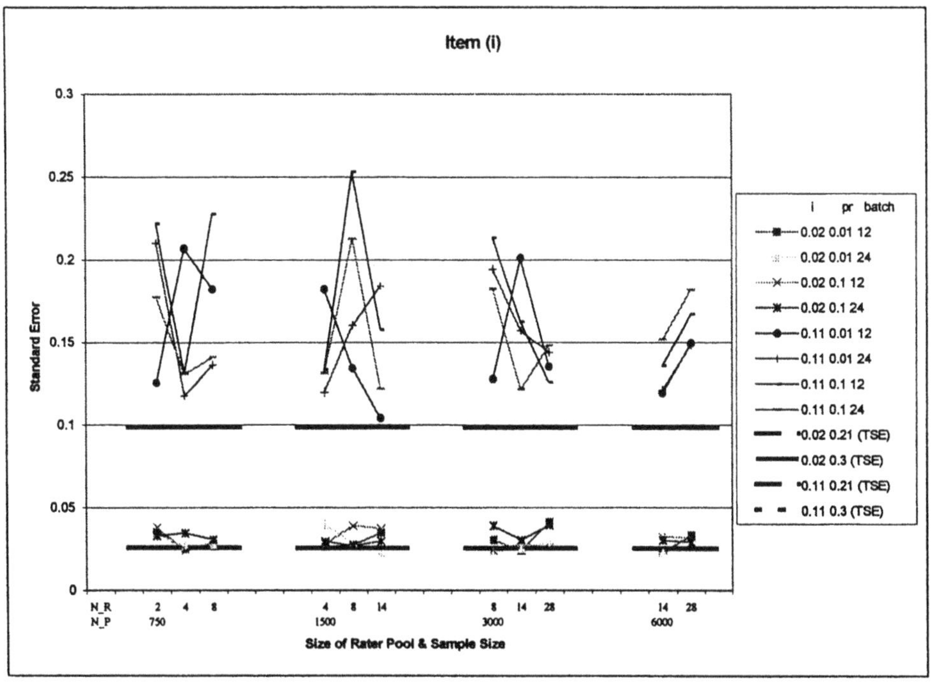

Figure 31: The randomness of the standard errors for the item effect (*connected mixture* rating plan).

4.8. ACCURACY AND PRECISION IN MAKING NORM- AND CRITERION- REFERENCED DECISIONS

4.8.1. Generalizability Coefficient

Both the generalizability and dependability coefficients were estimated with high accuracy (ACCURACY($E\rho^2$) and ACCURACY($\phi(\lambda)$) equaled 100% ± 1%) averaged across the 88 conditions. Figure 32 on page 91 shows the mean generalizability coefficients as a function of size of rater pool and sample size for low *item* and *person-by-rater* effects. The results resembled closely those for the high *item* and *person-by-rater* effects and thus only the low *item* effects were reported. The estimated generalizability coefficients were accurately estimated (population value = 0.6311) with sample sizes as small as 750 and they also retained properties as if they were estimated with complete data (i.e., the 95% confidence intervals became shorter as the sample size increased). Compared to the known values of the generalizability coefficients and their approximated theoretical confidence intervals, the empirical coefficients and confidence intervals were recovered within 0.003 of the theoretical predictions. See Figure 33 for the theoretical confidence intervals, which were obtained by the following steps: (1) compute the standard errors for each variance component (see Appendix B); (2) apply a multiplying factor (Brennan, 1992) to those variance components to find the upper and lower bound for each variance component; and (3) uses Equations (21) and (22) in section 3.7.4 to compute the confidence intervals for the coefficients.

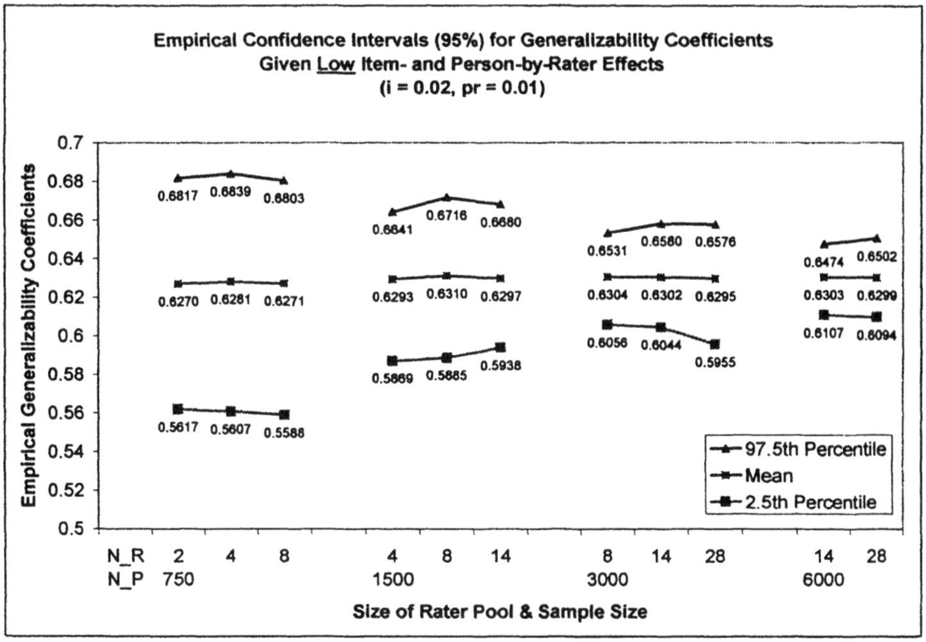

Figure 32: Empirical confidence intervals for generalizability coefficients.

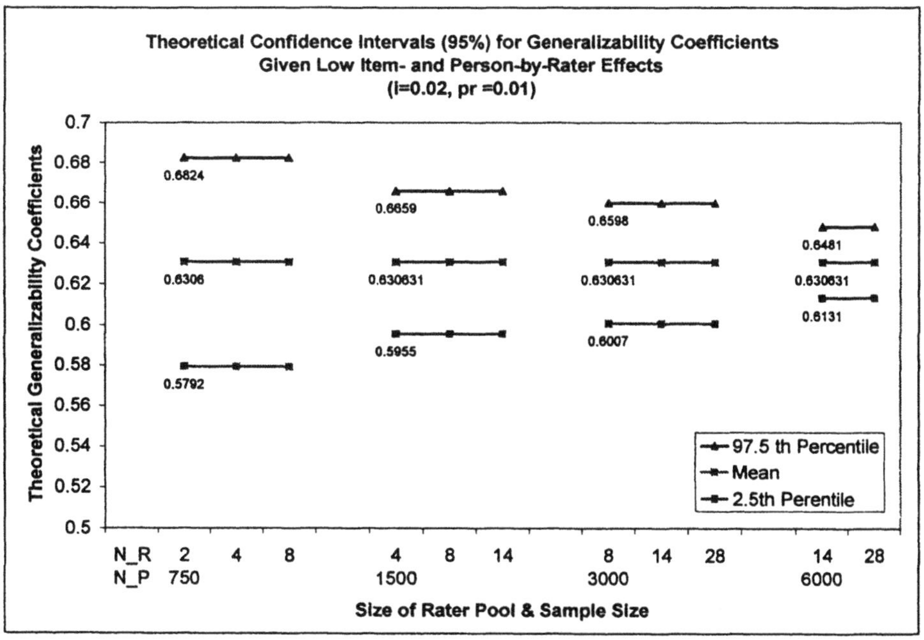

Figure 33: Theoretical generalizability coefficients.

4.8.2. Dependability Coefficient

The subdividing method was able to detect item variability for both high and low effects. The empirical dependability coefficients were close to the known parameter values and the corresponding confidence intervals were all recovered closely to the theoretical confidence intervals given low *item* effects (the average difference between the empirical and theoretical values was less than 0.0035). On average across the 88 conditions, the ACCURACY index of the dependability coefficients was 1.0 suggesting that the subdividing method provided unbiased estimates for the dependability coefficients (for any given one of the 88 conditions, the ACCURACY was 1.00 ± 0.03). For the high *item* effect, the lower bounds (2.5^{th} percentile) of the confidence intervals deviated farther from the mean than did the upper bounds (97.5^{th} percentile) indicating that one should be more confident in the upper bounds than the lower bounds of the dependability coefficients. Figure 35 on page 94 depicts this observation. Further investigations, discussed in the next paragraph, determined that the negatively skewed distribution of the empirical dependability coefficients reflected the unstable nature of the *item* effects due to large differences in item difficulties.

The theoretical lower bound of the dependability coefficient can be obtained by replacing the relative standard error of measurement with the absolute standard error of measurement in Equation (23). Holding sample size and the size of rater pool constant, the lower bound of the dependability coefficient became lower given any one or both of the following: (1) the lower limit of the effects for *item*, *rater*, *person-by-item*, *person-by-rater*, *item-by-rater*, or *person-by-item-rater, error* increases; and (2) the lower limit of the *object of measurement* decreases. An ad hoc study concluded that the skewed 2.5^{th} percentile of the dependability coefficients were caused by the highly variable *item* effect (at the high level =0.11), which had a maximum variance component of 1.57 and standard deviation 0.16 even though the mean of the high *item* effects was 0.11. The 2.5^{th} percentile of the dependability coefficients was raised by an average 14% when offsetting the estimated *item* effect variances in the high item effect conditions to the maximum of the estimated variances in the low *item* effect conditions (0.35). Notice that 0.35, which was at the 93th percentile on the high *item* and *person-by-rater* effect condition, was chosen to examine to what extent the lower bound of the dependability coefficient would rise when the extreme *item* effects were restricted to a lower value. Figure 34 shows the skewed distribution of the *item* effect.

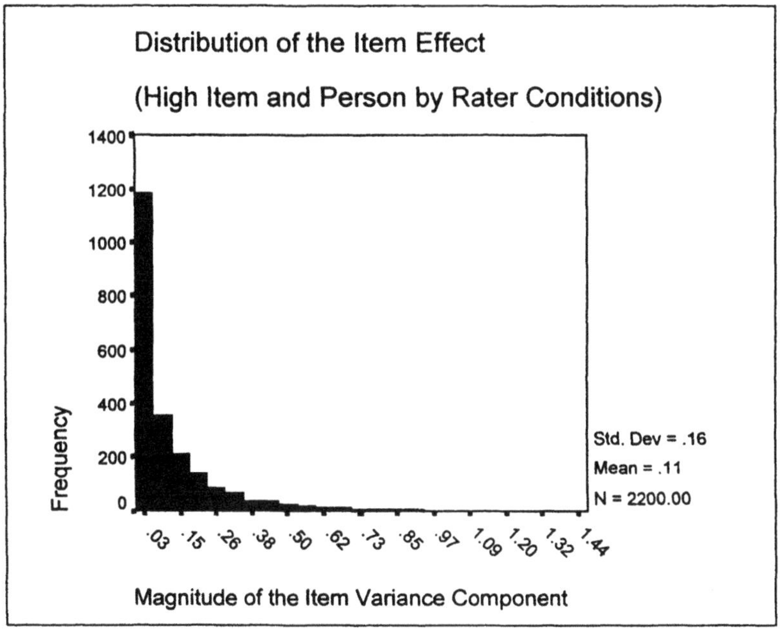

Figure 34: Distribution of the item variance components for the *disconnected crossed* rating plan (averaged across batch size, sample size, and rater pool size).

The boost of the 2.5th percentile of the dependability coefficients was depicted in Figure 35. This finding that the dependability coefficients became less skewed as the *item* effect became small substantiated that the subdividing method was capable of detecting various degrees of variability in generalizability studies.

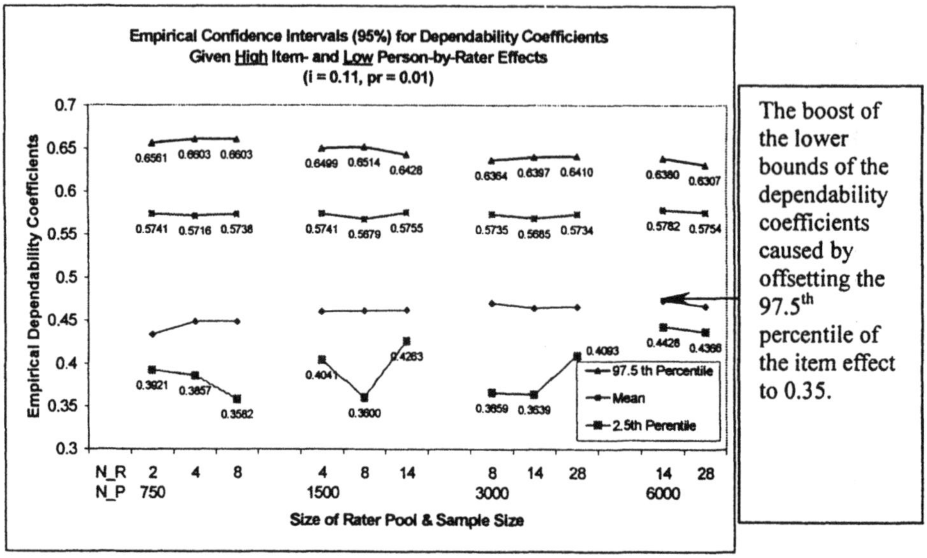

Figure 35: Dependability coefficients estimated in the *disconnected crossed* rating plan (high item effects).

Figure 36 shows that the confidence intervals of the dependability coefficients exhibited a narrowing trend as sample size increase for the low *item* effect conditions. The mean estimates of the dependability coefficients appeared to be rather stable and close to the known value (0.61135). Comparing those high *item* effect confidence intervals and estimates to low-*item*- effect conditions (see Figure 36), the 2.5th percentile of the dependability coefficients no longer appears to be so skewed when *item*-effect variation is low.

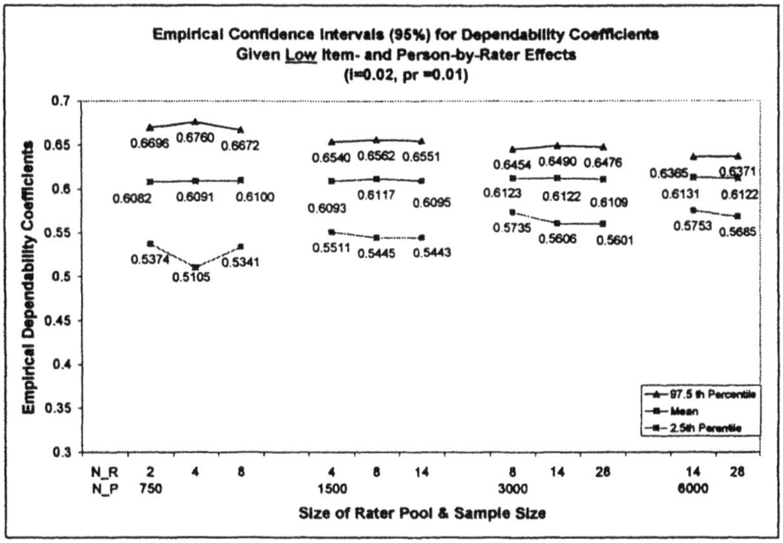

Figure 36: Dependability coefficients estimated in the *disconnected crossed* rating plan (low item effects).

4.8.3. Misclassification Error

Shown in Figure 37 were the estimates of the misclassification rates, with reference to the parameter values for the 88 conditions. They were computed based on the absolute standard error of measurement. Accuracy across all conditions was 100% ± 11% indicating that one would have made as few misclassification errors in unbalanced situations as one would in balanced situations. For instance, the error rate of misclassifying a random examinee with a true score 3.4 by one or more step was 1.70% given low *item* (0.02) and *person-by-rater* (0.11) effects in balanced situations (Table 7, page 50) whereas this error rate was 1.72% estimated by using the subdividing method for unbalanced situations. Given high *item* and *person-by-rater* effects, there was a 3.68% average misclassification rate in both balanced (Table 7) and unbalanced situations. Figure 38 shows the standard errors of the misclassification rates and it indicates that none of the standard errors of the 88 conditions exceeded 2.4%.

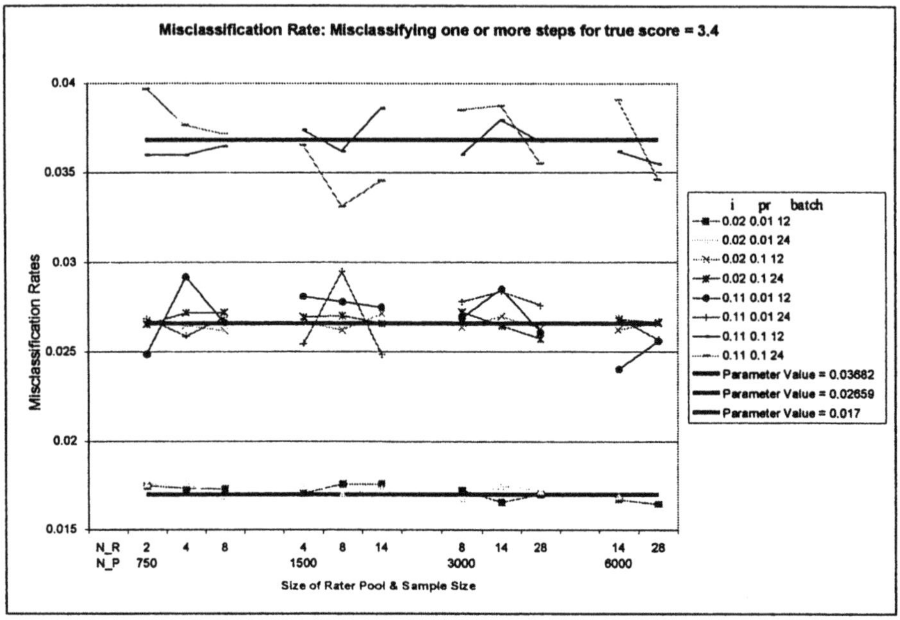

Figure 37: Misclassification error obtained for the *disconnected crossed* plan.

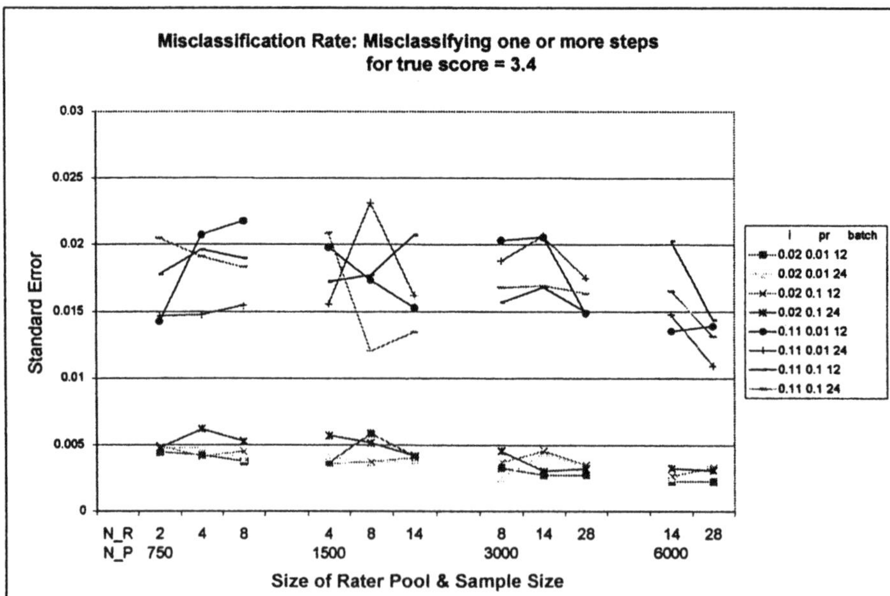

Figure 38: Standard errors of the misclassification rates for the *disconnected crossed* plan.

Chapter 5
CONCLUSIONS, DISCUSSIONS, AND FUTURE DIRECTIONS

5.1. SUBDIVIDING METHOD AND UNBALANCED SITUATIONS IN PERFORMANCE ASSESSMENT

Scoring constructed response items is more time consuming and complex than scoring multiple-choice items. Many educational and non-educational institutions adapt open-ended questions in examinations for admission, certification, graduation, accountability, and licensing purposes. These examinations often are administered on a large-scale basis. Large volumes of examinees are tested and yet only a short time (usually a few weeks) is available for scoring. Many raters are recruited to score the examinations and it is infeasible to assign all the raters to score every one of the examinees. Thus each examinee will be scored by a selection of raters, leading to sparsely-filled data sets and also unbalanced designs, and also causing potentially biased and imprecise estimators. The current monograph developed and validated a method, called the subdividing method, to resolve this problem. The subdividing method, drawing on the concept that one could obtain more stable estimators by synthesizing multiple data sources than using just one source, is set out to improve the accuracy and precision of estimates quantifying measurement errors in the framework of G theory. The implementation of this method was discussed in section 3.1.

The estimates produced by the subdividing method were scrutinized in determining how well the method worked in realistic scenarios (described in section 3.4 to 3.7) and these scenarios included differences in: (1) volume of examinees, (2) size of rater pool, (3) variation of item difficulty, (4) levels of rater inconsistency, (5) rules used to decide how to group raters and assign tasks to raters, and (6) the minimum number of examinees scored by a group of raters. Results in chapter 4 indicated that the subdividing method produced outcomes having properties (unbaisedness and consistency) that are similar to those of complete data methods. Different rules used for forming groups of raters changed the structural design of scores and thus influenced the precision of measurement error estimation. Unlike precision, the accuracy of estimating measurement errors was not as sensitive to the rules used for forming groups of raters. Accuracy of the outcomes was very high (close to perfect). These finding substantiated that the subdividing method produced unbiased outcomes with data missing completely at random. The section that follows summarizes major findings regarding the precision of estimators. Suggestions are provided for the set-up of scoring procedures.

5.2. MAJOR FINDINGS AND IMPLICATIONS

Weighting improved the precision of variances involving the person effect when data subsets varied in size. The standard errors of the weighted outcomes were closer to the theoretical standard errors when weights were applied (see section 4.1). As was discussed in section 3.2, data subsets varied in size in the *connected mixture* rating plan where there were more batches than possible groups of raters. Weighting, however, had no effect on the precision under the *disconnected crossed* rating plan, in which each group was composed of the same number of raters and each group scored the same number of examinees.

In large-scale performance assessments, examinees' work was packed in batches for scoring. Section 4.2 provided evidence that a minimum of 12 tasks scored by the same group of raters was sufficient to ensure precise estimates for the measurement errors, and increasing the minimum to 24 tasks did not tend to increase or lower the precision and the accuracy of measurements.

Results in section 4.3 suggested that the variance components, generalizability coefficient, dependability coefficient, and misclassification error were recovered by the subdividing method with high accuracy (100% ± 1%) in all experimental conditions examined for the two rating plans. Unlike the precision (inverse of standard errors) of variance components and composites, accuracy is not influenced by the patterns and amounts of missing data. This finding was consistent with the notion that when data are missing completely at random, one can still obtain an unbiased expected value but the standard error will be larger than that for a data set with no missing data (Little and Rubin, 1987).

In addition to the descriptive results reported in section 4.3, a multivariate regression (Rencher, 1995) was used to provide an omnibus test for the accuracy of the variance components. The results shown in Appendix H indicated that none of the predictors significantly deviated from zero (the five Wilks' Λs = 1.0 ± 0.001 and the corresponding p-values > 0.530), assuming normality. Table 24 (Appendix H) reports the value of the five individual Wilks' Λs. The regression coefficients and the coefficients of determination (r-squares) shown in Table 25 indicate that the subdividing method has estimated all the variance components with high accuracy (without biased) in all the experimental conditions. The intercepts were close to one, suggesting that the mean accuracy was close to 100%; the coefficients of the predictors were close to zero, showing that in no conditions did the accuracy of the subdividing method differ significantly. Even though the multivariate regression shed light on the accuracy of the subdividing method, this analysis provides only supplementary information to those analyses reported in section 4.3. One should interpret the results of the regression analysis with caution because the multivariate normality assumptions were not completely met by all the variance components (e.g., the *item* component had a positively skewed distribution).

Frequently, the number of raters recruited to score examinees has an inverse relationship to the time available for completing the scoring, holding the volume of examinees constant. The section entitled Amounts and Patterns of Missing Data (p. 44) indicated that expanding the rater pool required more raters to provide more stable estimates for the rater-related effects, but the expansion of the rater pool induced more unobserved data. To what degree can the gain in precision by using more raters compensate for the decrease in precision due to the increasing amounts of unobserved data? Section 4.4 reported that doubling the rater pool increased the precision of estimating the *rater* effect and the *item-by-rater* effect by at most 32%. This finding was consistent with the expectation that more raters leads to higher precision of estimating the rater effect, provided that the raters came from the same population. Similarly, the same conclusions applied to the *item-by-rater* effect. Thus even though it is infeasible to have raters completely crossed with examinees, it is still desirable to use more raters rather than fewer raters, because this will result in characterizing the rater effects with higher confidence.

Results in 4.4 revealed that the theoretical $SE(\hat{\sigma}_r^2)$ was lower than the empirical $SE(\hat{\sigma}_r^2)$ given a small rater pool (i.e., the two-rater condition). With the following rationales, one can see that the theoretical method underestimated the precision of the *rater* and *item-by-rater* facets for extremely small sample sizes, while the empirical method provided estimates with the right degree of precision. First, one can rule out the argument that the empirical standard errors were incorrectly estimated because the empirical standard errors resembled closely the theoretical standard errors for the other effects, namely $SE(\hat{\sigma}_p^2)$, $SE(\hat{\sigma}_{pi}^2)$, $SE(\hat{\sigma}_{pr}^2)$, and $SE(\hat{\sigma}_{pir,e}^2)$. Second, theoretical standard errors for statistics require asymptotic assumptions that may be inaccurate (Smith, 1982). In the present case, we used two and four levels, respectively, for the *rater-* and *item-by-rater* effects. For this reason, it is likely that the theoretical standard errors were too small.

Given a desirable level of precision obtained by sampling from a pool of raters, how many raters are needed to obtain the same level of precision for $\hat{\sigma}_r^2$ without sampling? Table 16 in section 4.4 shows the answers to this question. Whether or not the theoretical SE was underestimated for small numbers of raters, the numbers of raters needed to match the precision obtained in the sampling situation would be fewer than predicted in Table 16 for the *rater* effect. For instance, one may need to use all 13 raters at the most to score examinees in order to match the level of precision of the *rater* effect yielded by sampling two raters from a pool of 28.

The size of rater pool had little influence on the precision of the *person-by-rater* effect (Figure 22, section 4.4) for the *disconnected crossed* rating plan. No matter how large the rater pool, $SE(\hat{\sigma}_{pr}^2)$ tended to stay at the level equivalent to that obtained by using two raters. The empirical standard errors clustered around the theoretical values of $SE(\hat{\sigma}_{pr}^2)$ and the fluctuation was rather subtle. One explanation was that as the rater pool size expanded the percentage of unobserved data also increased. On the one hand, expanding rater size pool gave more information about the degree to which raters scored examinees differently. On the other hand, expanding the rater pool size while keeping the same number of ratings for each task caused less observed data to be allocated for estimating the *person-by-rater* effect. The tension between these two factors (increasing rater pool size and increasing amounts of unobserved data) tended to compensate for one another. This finding suggested that employing more raters did not tend to lower or boost the precision of characterizing the *person-by-rater* effect, holding sample size constant and assuming raters came from the same population.

The finding that $SE(\hat{\sigma}_{pr}^2)$ was inversely related to the volume of examinees suggested that the subdividing method led to consistent estimators (section 4.5). Practically, this is a desirable property to have for large-scale testing because it enables one to apply the G theory framework to partition measurement errors with high confidence as more examinees are assessed.

With 6000 examinees, $SE(\hat{\sigma}^2_{pr})$ was in the range 0.002 to 0.005. With 750 examinees, $SE(\hat{\sigma}^2_{pr})$ was in the neighborhood of 0.01 and 0.013.

Typically, scoring centers do not have much control over the volume of examinees — less control than on the number of raters to be employed. A feasible way to improve the precision of $\hat{\sigma}^2_{pr}$ is to employ rating plans that ensure plenty of data to be used for the estimation of $SE(\hat{\sigma}^2_{pr})$. Although the *disconnected crossed* rating plan (section 4.6) examined in the current research allowed one to utilize all the data to estimate $SE(\hat{\sigma}^2_{pr})$, this rating plan was designed to estimate the *person-by-rater* effect using non-overlapping groups of raters (i.e., groups of raters were *disconnected*). With another rating plan that allocates data to examine both the overlapping and non-overlapping rater groups, one would expect to improve $SE(\hat{\sigma}^2_{pr})$. Such a rating plan could guarantee all the data subsets to exhibit the *crossed* design while allowing raters to be on more than one scoring committee. This rating plan is constituted of three rules listed as follows.

$$rater_{i,t,s} \neq rater'_{i,t,s} \tag{24}$$

$$rater_{t,s} = rater_{t,s+1} \tag{25}$$

$$rater'_{t,s} \neq rater'_{t,s+1} \tag{26}$$

The first rule, Equation (24), ensures that no rater scores an examinee on the same item (i) twice in a given data subset (s) of the *crossed* design. The second rule (25) indicates that all raters participated in exactly two scoring groups, namely the sth *and* $s+1^{th}$ groups. The third rule (26) specifies that all raters worked with a different rater in the two groups they sit in. This rating plan can be called the *connected crossed* rating plan. The shaded areas in the following figure show the observed data and it can be seen that every group of raters has a common linking rater with one other group. Future research is needed to compare this *connected crossed* rating plan with those two examined in the current study.

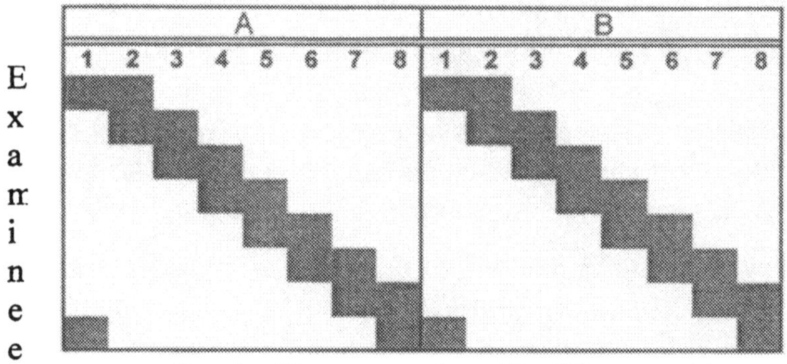

Note: A and B represent two items; "1" to "8" represent eight raters.

Figure 39: A hypothetical *connected crossed* rating plan.

Unlike the results found for the *disconnected crossed* rating plan, the precision of the *person-by-rater* effect decreased as the rater pool size expanded in the *connected mixture* rating plan (section 4.6). The loss of precision was due to fewer data points being allocated to the *crossed* and the *MBIB* structural designs. These results suggested a general principle for designing rating plans — rating plans with loose structure and fewer guiding rules (e.g., the *connected mixture* rating plan was less structured than the *disconnected crossed* rating plan) tend to form data subsets with *nested* rather than *crossed* structural designs. For this reason, very few data sets were available to estimate the *rater* effect separately from the *item* effects. The larger the rater pool and the less structured the rating plan, the less precisely one can estimate the rater-related effects. A recommendation based on this finding suggests that one should impose structural designs at the data subset level and the structural designs chosen should be geared toward to the effects of interest.

The results in section 4.8 showing that the dependability coefficient had an asymmetric 95% confidence interval with an extended tail towards the low end has implications for developing and scoring performance based assessments. First, even though the *item* effect accounted for only approximately 11% (σ_i^2 = 0.11) of the total score variation, its variance component had a wide confidence interval because only two items were used to estimate its large population value. Empirically, the overall 95% CI was between 0 and 0.627 with a mean standard error 0.157, which was larger than the population value. Since the *item* effect component was used in the denominator of the dependability coefficient, it then dragged down the lower bound of the dependability coefficient. The upper bound of the dependability coefficient was not affected because the *item* facet has a positive skewed distribution implying that the lower bound of the *item* facet was not as influential as the upper bound. For this reason, the wide confidence interval of the dependability coefficient was contributed to largely by the *item* effect. The subdividing method provides a means to characterize this skewed-dependability phenomenon in unbalanced situations. Such a wide confidence interval is expected in balanced situations as this can be demonstrated by comparing the dependability coefficients obtained by a large and a small σ^2_Δ in Equation (32). As was illustrated in section 4.8, reducing either $SE(\sigma^2_i)$ or σ^2_i itself could provide a more dependable measurement procedure for making criterion-referenced decisions. In fact, many researchers (e.g., Bejar, 1993) have developed methods to control for item variation and to increase the generalizability of tasks (e.g., Kane, Crooks, and Cohen, 1999).

5.3. NEW APPLICATIONS OF THE SUBDIVIDING METHOD AND FUTURE DIRECTIONS

(I) The current research examined the statistical properties of recovered variance components under a two faceted design, namely the *person* x *item* x *rater* design. The rater facet was sampled, but the facet to be sampled could be the *item* or any one facet in a two faceted design. The subdividing method can be used to examine the generalizability for a measurement procedure where examinees respond to a complete set of questions (as opposed to a subsample from that complete set of questions). Such a comparison can be accomplished by finding out the precision of generalizability in unbalanced situations (e.g., via resampling or bootstrapping methods) and then using that level of precision as a target for predicting how many raters and /or items are needed to maintain the target level of precision in a balanced situation. Such applications can be useful to reduce testing time while being able to evaluate the quality of the testing procedures. To determine the potential results for this application where examinees responded to only a selected set of items and were scored by all raters, one can simply swap the subscripts between the *item* and *rater* effects in the results section of the current book. Having examinees to respond to only a set of items from a pool of items can reduce testing time. Having all raters to score examinees can become feasible in the future as testing companies such as the Educational Testing Service (ETS) are developing artificial-intelligence and natural language processing technology to use computer programs (called electronic raters or e-raters), which are designed to reduce human scoring (Bennett, 2001; Brennan, 2000; Personal communication from Bejar, 1999 and Hombo, 1999).

The *Subdividing* method is equipped to evaluate the quality of ratings provided by "e-rater", because it is easy to envision that test developers may desire to try out a number of scoring algorithms or rubrics on the "e-rater" before putting a test in operation. Since scoring algorithms or rubrics are developed by experts, variations should exist among the algorithms. Given the availability of many programs, it will be time consuming to score every examinee by all possible scoring algorithms and rubrics. This constraint is analogous to using a large pool of human raters to score every single examinee. Such a scenario will result in an unbalanced design, for which the score reliability can be evaluated using the *Subdividing* method.

Another application of the subdividing method is to evaluate any systematic measurement procedures involving observations and ratings where data are unbalanced, such as alternate assessments that might be used for special education students in place of traditional assessments (Ysseldyke & Olsen, 1999). In addition, the subdividing method can be applied to any large-scale assessments such as state assessments and the National Assessment of Educational Progress (NAEP).

(II) The subdividing method developed in the current study was examined using two common rating plans. In operation, scoring sessions may not document explicitly the rating plans used. In that case, it is researchers' hope rather than expectation to have the data collected in the same way as data would be collected by the rating plans. An *index of sparseness* indicating the pattern and the extent to which scores were unobserved (e.g., as compared to those in the specified plans) may be useful. Such an index requires future development. Graphical displays and research on matrix analysis (Alan & Liu, 1981) can give insight to this line of development.

(III) A follow-up study investigating the specific principles (p. 48) used in different rating plans will be invaluable. The current study examined the *disconnected crossed* and *connected mixture* rating plans. These two plans differed in several ways (see Table 6 for comparisons) and future studies should be conducted to isolate each of the underlying principles distinguishing these and other rating plans. One such principle, namely the guiding structural designs within a given group (the third principle in Table 6) can provide practical insight for test developers. How does having the same set of raters score all the tasks from an examinee (crossed design) as opposed to having different sets of raters to score different tasks (mixture designs or nested designs) influence the quality of the scoring procedures? Patz (1999) spoke in favor of using stratified designs when applying Item Response Theory (IRT) models to analyze performance-based data. He stated that stratified designs allow different sets of raters to score the different tasks submitted by an examinee and thus the chance for an examinee to receive scores from solely a set of extreme raters (either too lenient or harsh) will be lower than using a crossed design. Kane, Crooks, and Cohen (1999, p.14) also suggested that "having each task evaluated by a different set of scorers" can increase the number of raters evaluating each student and thus helps to control any lack of consistency among raters. Although stratified or non-crossed structures, like that suggested by Kane, Crooks, and Cohen (1999) and Patz (1999), have the advantage to ensure that each student's task is scored by a larger number of raters than in a crossed structure, they do not necessarily allow one to disentangle rater-related interaction effects. So, one may not be able to evaluate as precisely the rater-related interactions (e.g., the *rater x item* effect) as one can in a crossed structure. Since a line of research studying rating plans and the statistical properties of reliability and dependability coefficients is emerging, more research should be conducted (Glick and Picou, 1999; Patz, 1999; and Wilson, 1999). Comparing the *connected mixture* rating plan studied in the current monograph and the *connected crossed* rating plan proposed on page 102 can shed light on methods to scoring performance-based questions with high generalizability and dependability. One can find more examples of different rating plans in other areas of the measurement literature such as test equating (Kolen & Brennan, 1995).

(IV) Future research may examine factors in addition to those investigated in the current study such as the degree to which data are not missing completely at random. In practice, some raters (e.g. more experienced) may score more responses than the others. In this scenario, data may not be missing completely at random because some raters have more unobserved data while others have less. Put differently, missing data were related to the experience of the raters. Little and Rubin (1987) called this data Missing At Random (MAR). In applying the subdividing method to the MAR scenario, one can weight the data subset by the experience of the raters (which can be operationalized as the number of responses scored) in the Synthesizing stage. Future studies are needed in evaluating the subdividing method in such scenario.

(V) The current study applied a multivariate regression to predict the accuracy of the variance components using the experimental factors controlled in the simulation as predictors. The inferential results should be treated as tentative, as the skewed distributions of the variance components did not satisfy completely the multivariate normal assumptions. The low parameter values used for the *item* and *rater* effects caused these variance components to have a distribution with negative values, which prevented one from using logarithmic transformations to normalize the variance components (e.g., transformation suggested by Kalaian & Becker, 1996 and Raudenbush, 1988). Exploring transformations with known statistical properties for negative variance components deserves much attention; this line of research will be invaluable for the measurement community because it can provide correct inferential conclusions about measurement procedures.

(VI) Though G theory is popular for disentangling multiple sources of variation in scores, it does so via the expected variation for each facet. It does not, however, identify individual elements contributing to the variations (e.g., G theory does not indicate which individual rater is particularly more lenient or severe as compared to the other raters). A thorough diagnosis utilizing methods such as cluster analysis and meta-analysis goodness of fit tests can examine individual elements more closely and diagnose problems in the measurement procedures more carefully.

5.4. SUGGESTIONS TO TEST DEVELOPERS AND EDUCATIONAL VALUES

5.4.1. Suggestions to Test Developers

The results of the current research study inform discussions of scoring procedures for performance assessment. Is there a particular scoring arrangement that can yield more accurate and stable estimates for measurement errors than other arrangements? The current monograph showed that the *disconnected crossed* produced more precise estimates for the *person-by-rater* effect than the *connected mixture* rating plan. Also, given the same sized rater pool, how many examinees must be scored by the same group of raters in order to provide precise evaluations of measurement error? A minimum of 12 examinees scored by the same group of raters was sufficient to ensure precise estimates for the measurement errors. Increasing that minimum to 24 examinees did not tend to increase or lower the precision of measurement errors. This finding suggests to test developers that bundling tasks is not a real concern as far as measurement errors go. Given the resources and time, test developers should, instead, consider seriously what rating plan to use in order to reduce measurement errors and to obtain an accurate and precise portrait of those errors. Rating plans should be chosen prior to starting a scoring session to structure and randomize the data collection procedures (scoring procedures).

When conducting generalizability analyses, test developers should apply weights for combining the measurement errors estimated from each data subset. At the best, weighting will increase the precision of characterizing the quality of a measurement procedure and in no situation will it lower the precision. However, one does not necessarily need to apply weights in using the subdividing method for generalizability analyses provided that the data subset sizes are equal. Data subsets have equal sample sizes when one employs the *disconnected crossed* rating plan. Section 3.2 of this book provides decision rules and formulae to determine the need for weighting with the *connected mixture* rating plan. By and large, it is more likely that one needs to apply weights when a small pool of raters (e.g, four raters) scores a large volume of examinees (e.g., 1500) than when a larger pool of raters (e.g., eight raters) scores the same volume of examinees.

The results reported in this book suggested that the use of only a few items varying much in mean difficulty was a major source of variance, lowering the dependability of a measurement procedure and thus leading to unreliable criterion-referenced decisions. A well thought-out rating plan can help one confidently determine more rater-related measurement errors but it does not help more confidently determine the difference in mean item difficulty (i.e., *item* effect). Increasing the rater pool or sample size did not affect the estimation of the *item* effect in unbalanced situations when the subdividing method was employed. Although administering more items to examinees can reduce the *item* effect and increase its associated confidence interval, this may not be a feasible resolution because adding more performance-based items to a test will increase testing time and costs to the education system and it will also burden the students. Increasing the homogeneity of test items is an alternative to improve the dependability of a measurement procedure. This can be achieved by writing items similar in difficulty. A second alternative is to shorten the length of performance-based tasks so that more tasks could be administered in a limited testing time. A third alternative is to "increase the correlation among task scores by avoiding tasks that require esoteric information or that involve some unique format" (Kane, Crooks, and Cohen, 1999, p. 14).

Test developers frequently have to report scores in a short time. For instance, the Mathematics and Sciences tests of the 1996 National Assessment of Educational Progress (NAEP) employed 675 raters to score 8,985,583 constructed responses in 12 1/2 weeks (Authors, 1996). The sooner the test developers need to complete scoring an examination, the more raters they need to recruit. It was shown that the subdividing method can detect the *rater* and *item-by-rater* effects more precisely as the size of rater pool increases, holding everything else constant. If test developers recruit more raters and obtained a considerably larger *rater* effect than they obtained before increasing the rater pool, they can be certain that the mean scores assigned by the additional raters are more variable than those assigned by the original pool of raters (i.e., the new raters may be more lenient or harsh than the original raters). Likewise, any large increase in the *item-by-rater* effect due to expanding the rater pool size indicates that the additional raters exhibited a higher degree of inconsistency in scoring items differentially than did the original group of raters.

Testing agencies should be mindful of choosing a rating plan at the same time they consider increasing the size of a rater pool. The chosen rating plan influences the precision of quantifying measurement errors and thus the generalizability and the dependability of a measurement procedure. If test developers use the *connected mixture* rating plan and decide to recruit more raters to score the same number of examinees, test developers ought to anticipate that they will obtain less stable estimates for the *rater*, *item-by-rater*, *person-by-rater*, and *person-by-item-by-rater* effects than they would with fewer raters. The reduction of precision occurs because, as the rater pool size expands, fewer data are allocated to the *crossed* and *MBIB* designs for estimating those effects separately from one another. The data are instead allocated to the *nested* design, which does not estimate the all the effects in the *crossed* and *MBIB* designs. Alternatively, if test developers need to use the *connected mixture* rating plan for logistic reasons, they may consider converting estimates from the *crossed* and *MBIB* designs to match the estimates from the *nested* design in order to utilize all the data for obtaining precise estimates. The *rater-nested-in-item* effect, in the *nested* design, becomes an upper bound for either the *rater* or the *item-by-rater* effects in the *crossed* and *MBIB* designs. By the same token, the *person-by-rater-nested-in-item* effect becomes the upper bound for the *person-by-rater* or the *person-by-item-by-rater* effects in the *crossed* and *MBIB* designs. If test developers provide extensive training and monitoring to the raters with anticipation that both the *rater-nested-in-item* and *person-by-rater-nested-in-item* effects will be low in magnitude, the *connected mixture* rating plan can be used. This is because the expansion in rater pool will increase the precision of the measurement error estimates, as the *connected mixture* rating plan allocates all data to estimate the effects in a *nested* design.

With computer technology, the implementation of different rating plans becomes easier. Examinees' constructed responses (e.g., essays) can be scanned into digital format and raters can score these responses on-line so that they can focus on scoring rather than paper routing. Computer technology enables test developers to have full control to structure scoring sessions and this enables them to implement a desirable rating plan prior to using the subdividing method to analyze unbalanced data. The subdividing method always requires less computational power than other methods that analyze the entire sparsely-filled data set. For example, instead of analyzing a data set of 6000 examinees and 28 raters all at once, one can parse this unbalanced data into subsets, analyze each subset, and then synthesize the results from the subsets. The subdividing method enhances the scoring procedures for rating constructed-response items and it serves as a means to prepare performance assessments to be reliably used in large-scale settings.

5.4.2. Educational Values

Given the proliferation of performance assessments, many states and school districts have already implemented this type of assessment on a regular basis. Well-developed scoring rubrics can be useful, provided that raters implement them consistently and accurately. Large-scale performance-based assessments can be used for accountability purposes only if methods are developed to evaluate the quality of the scoring procedures (Mehrens,1992). Training raters to consistently apply the scoring criteria described in the rubrics designed for large-scale performance assessments, has many instructional benefits. When raters (mostly school teachers) return to their classrooms, they will be accustomed to using those criteria.

Improving the quality of performance assessment so that it can be used for high-stakes decisions also can help align assessments with curriculum and instruction (Pearson, 1998). Many researchers such as Bracey (1989) reported that schools and teachers were less likely to include materials in their classrooms if the materials would not be tested in high-stakes examinations. Developing methods to monitor and improve the quality of performance assessment could reduce the tensions in using this state-of-the-art assessment for classroom instruction and for high-stakes decisions. Students will be the beneficiaries of this development, which was examined in the current monograph.

Chapter 6
COMPUTER PROGRAMS AND RATER DESIGN DIAGNOSIS

In this chapter, we describe a computer program to implement the subdividing method (see Chapter 3) and two utility programs to automate large-scale simulations. As was discussed in Chapters 2 and 3, variance component estimations for the applications of Generalizability theory analysis can be too intensive even for powerful computers. Although the subdividing method can overcome this limitation, it is a labor-intensive task to manually implement the method. To this end, the *Subdividing Program* is developed. It is an add-on module that runs on SPSS® (Windows versions). Specifically, the *Subdividing Program* has three major functionalities that it can: (a) divide up a large sparsely filled data set into small subsets; (b) estimate the variance components of each subset; and (c) diagnose the underlying essay-rater distribution process. Each of the above functionalities will produce an output in SPSS. In this chapter, two examples will be used to illustrate these functionalities as well as to provide a context for an in-depth interpretation of the output. Special attention will be devoted to the interpretations of the essay-rater distribution process, denoted *rater profile* hereafter, which is central to the missing data patterns in large-scale assessments.

While the *Subdividing Program* receives the most attention in this chapter, a limited discussion will be devoted for the two utility programs, which evolved from the current simulation study. Regardless that these two programs were designed to facilitate the validation process of the subdividing method, they are general enough for the immediate use of many other types of research. For example, one can use these programs to conduct a large-scale simulation project searching for optimal rater designs. These programs can be used as a standalone program independently of the substantive research questions. One can take advantage of these flexible programs so long as multiple computers are used and multiple files were created.

6.1. ILLUSTRATIONS OF THE SPSS SUBDIVIDING PROGRAM

The *Subdividing Program* was tested in version 10.0.7 of SPSS. It runs on earlier versions that support scripting and macros (SPSS 10.0 Developer's Guide). Once installed, it will appear on the pull-down menu of SPSS. Two stages are involved in running the program, namely the setup and the file selection stages. Users first activate the program in the setup stage (Figure 40). They then supply the name of the data file to be analyzed in the second stage (Figure 41). Two sets of results will be generated subsequently in the output screen of SPSS. The first set of results will contain the data subset information, which indicates the identification of rater groups who scored a common set of essays. Not only does it displays the workload for each rater group, but it also shows the diagnostic information for the mechanism used to distribute essays to raters. For example, the table shows if the raters work in independent groups; to whom raters teamed up to score the essays; and whether each rater group scored all or just one of the essays submitted by examinees. The second set of output produced by the *Subdividing Program* displays the modified output of the variance component module (SPSS Advanced Statistics 7.5). Specifically, it displays the variance component estimates for each data subset shown in Table 22.

The next section delineates the interpretations of the two sets of outputs. Two examples are selected to show the variety of possible outputs. The first and second examples show the outputs from a *disconnected crossed* and a *connected mixture* structure, respectively, which were discussed in the previous chapters.

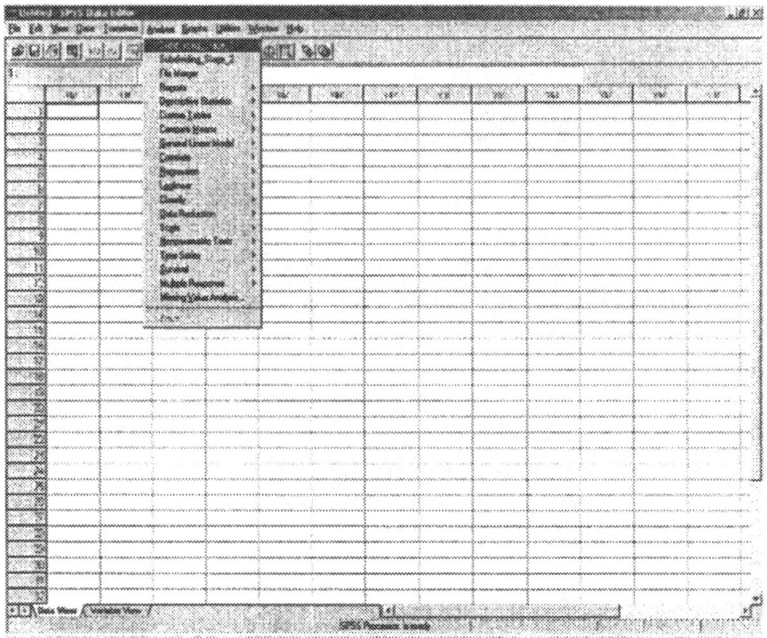

Figure 40: Program activation.

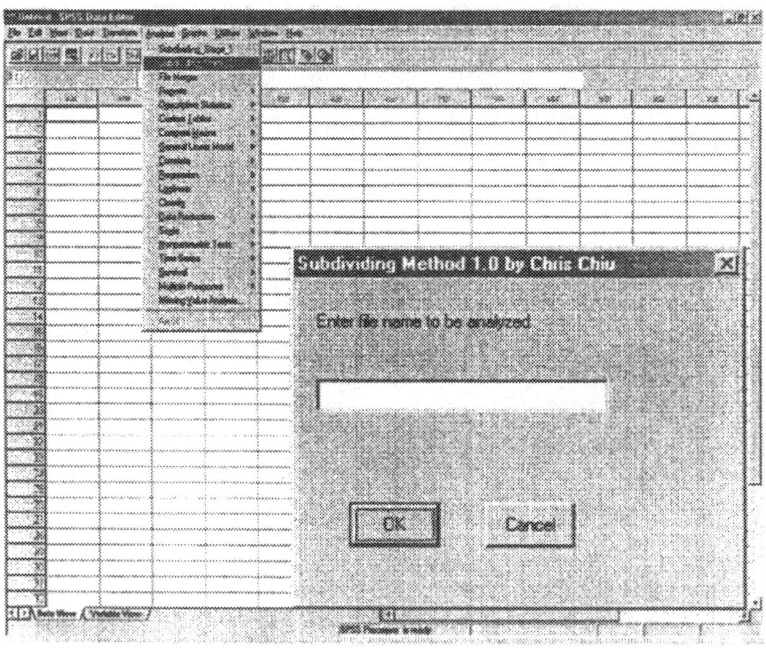

Figure 41: Dialog box to use the subdividing program.

6.1.1. Example 1

Summary of Hypothetical Data

We used the mechanism described in Chapter 3 to generate a sparsely filled data set exhibiting a *disconnected crossed* structure. Seven hundred and fifty hypothetical examinees were simulated. Each of them submitted two essays for assessments and both essays were rated two times to ensure scoring consistency. Two independent raters gave the two ratings. As a result, 3000 responses were collected (750 examinees X 2 essays X 2 ratings). A "double scoring" rule was also used to ensure that once a rater was selected to score an essay for an examinee, s/he also scored the other essay of the same examinee. In addition, essays were bundled in batches of 12 before they were randomly distributed to the raters. Because of the random process, the raters were expected to have similar workload. Table 20 summarizes the hypothetical data.

Table 20: Summary Table for the Scoring Process

Number of Examinees	Number of Essays submitted by each examinee	Number of times that each essay was graded	Total Essays Graded	Number of Raters
750	2	2	3000	8

Results of the Subdividing Program

We applied the *Subdividing Program* to analyze the simulated data set. The structure of the data set appeared to confirm the model used to generate the data. Table 21 displays the diagnosis of the data structure. Column one indicates that the entire group of examinees was divided into four groups or subsets. A completely different rater pair scored each of the four groups. The first column in Table 21 also shows the rater pairs for the four groups. For instance, raters 1 and 3 scored examinee group one and raters 2 and 8 scored group two. The second column in Table 21 indicates the workload of the rater pairs, in the unit of essays. Raters 1 and 3, as a group denoted "D1D3" scored 744 essays, which were composed by 186 examinees (186 examinees X 2 essays X 2 ratings = 744). By the same token, the second and third rater pairs scored the same number of essays. The workload for the last pair was slightly heavier (768 essays). On average, the four pairs each scored approximately the same percentage of essays (25% ± 1%), as shown in the third column. As shown in the last column, no essays were left unscored (100%).

Table 21: Diagnosis of Rater-Essay Distribution Process (Subdividing Program Output)

Rater Identification

			Number of Essays Scored	Percent	Cumulative Percent
Data Subsets	1	D1D3 [a]	744	24.8	24.8
	2	D2D8	744	24.8	49.6
	3	D4D5	744	24.8	74.4
	4	D6D7	768	25.6	100.0
	Total		3000	100.0	

a. Footnote: The letter "D" indicates that the associated rater provided double scoring to the examinees (i.e., the raters scored the examinees twice, once on each item). For instance, "D1D3" represents that raters 1 and 3 scored the same group of examinees on two items.

Another output of the *Subdividing Program* was the Variance Component Table, which reports the unweighted estimates of variance components for each of the data subsets (see Table 22) below. We can obtain an overall estimate of the variance components by weighting each estimates by the sample size of the data subsets. Specifically, the aggregated variance component for the *object of measurement* is 0.3504 ($\Sigma f_s(x) \bullet \hat{\sigma}_s^2(p)$ = 0.248*0.329 + 0.248*0.407 + 0.248*0.456 + 0.256*0.214). The aggregated variance component was very close to the population parameter used to simulate the hypothetical data (i.e., 0.35).

Table 22: Variance Component Estimates for Data Subsets (Subdividing Program Output)

Data Subsets	Estimated Components						
	p	i	r	pi	pr	ir	pir,e
D1D	.329	.156	.005	.259	.014	.000 [a]	.229
D2D	.407	.154	.011	.306	.038	.000 [a]	.171
D4D	.456	.113	.010	.241	.012	.002	.207
D6D	.214	.269	.005	.384	.035	.013	.187

a. The negative variance component estimates were set to zero.

6.1.2. Example 2

Summary of Hypothetical Data

We used the method described in Chapter 3 to generate a sparsely filled data set exhibiting a *connected mixture* structure. A completely new group of seven hundred and fifty hypothetical examinees was used. The data set was simulated using a similar procedure as used in Example 1. The primary difference is that the "double scoring" rule was not used in the current example. Consequently, the same raters did not necessarily score two essays per examinee.

Results of the Subdividing Program

We applied the *Subdividing Program* to analyze the simulated data set. Table 22 displays the resulting output of the data, which was subdivided into 60 smaller subsets. Each subset was associated with a markup label indicating the raters chosen for the subset. For simplicity, we provide a brief interpretation of these labels in the current paragraph and save the thorough interpretation for the next section. As shown, only two subsets were doubly scored (subset IDs 7 and 10), in which the "double raters" scored both items of the same examinees; 33 subsets exhibited a nested structural design in which two completely different raters were selected to score the two items (e.g., subset IDs 13 and 14); 25 exhibited an *Modified Balanced Incomplete Block* structure (discussed in the previous chapter), where one rater scored two items and a completely different pair was chosen to provide a second rating on the two items (e.g., subset IDs 1 and 2). Table 22 also shows that the majority of the rater groups (93.3%) scored 48 essays. Only three groups (5%) scored 96 essays and one group (1.67%) scored 24 essays. The output table of the variance component estimates for this example is suppressed as it resembles that of the previous example.

Table 23: Diagnosis of Rater-Essay Distribution Process for Example Two (Output from the Subdividing Program)

Rater Identification				
Subset ID	Data Subsets (Rater Groups)	Number of Essays Scored by Each Rater Group	Percent	Cumulative Percent
1	D1S4aS7b	48	1.6	1.6
2	D1S4bS8a	48	1.6	3.2
3	D1S5bS7a	96	3.2	6.4
4	D1S5bS8a	48	1.6	8
5	D2S5bS6a	48	1.6	9.6
6	D2S5bS7a	48	1.6	11.2
7	D3D4	48	1.6	12.8
8	D3S4aS8b	48	1.6	14.4
9	D3S4bS7a	48	1.6	16
10	D5D8	48	1.6	17.6
11	D5S6bS8a	48	1.6	19.2
12	S1aS2bD5	48	1.6	20.8
13	S1aS2bS3bS5a	48	1.6	22.4
14	S1aS2bS5bS8a	48	1.6	24
15	S1aS2bS6aS8b	48	1.6	25.6
16	S1aS3bS4bS5a	48	1.6	27.2
17	S1aS3bS5aS6b	48	1.6	28.8
18	S1aS3bS5bS7a	48	1.6	30.4
19	S1aS3bS6aS8b	48	1.6	32
20	S1aS4bS7aS8b	48	1.6	33.6
21	S1bD3S5a	48	1.6	35.2
22	S1bS2aS3bS5a	96	3.2	38.4
23	S1bS2aS4bS5a	48	1.6	40
24	S1bS4aD7	48	1.6	41.6
25	S1bS5aS7aS8b	48	1.6	43.2
26	S2aD5S8b	48	1.6	44.8
27	S2aS3bS4aS8b	48	1.6	46.4
28	S2aS3bS4bS8a	48	1.6	48
29	S2aS3bS5aS8b	48	1.6	49.6
30	S2aS3bS5bS7a	48	1.6	51.2
31	S2aS4bS5aS6b	48	1.6	52.8
32	S2aS4bS7bS8a	48	1.6	54.4
33	S2aS7bD8	48	1.6	56
34	S2bS3aD7	48	1.6	57.6
35	S2bS3aS4bS7a	48	1.6	59.2
36	S2bS3aS5aS7b	48	1.6	60.8
37	S2bS3aS6bS7a	48	1.6	62.4
38	S2bS3bS7aS8a	48	1.6	64
39	S2bS4aD6	48	1.6	65.6
40	S2bS5aS7aS8b	48	1.6	67.2
41	S2bS7aD8	48	1.6	68.8
42	S3aD5S7b	48	1.6	70.4
43	S3aD6S7b	48	1.6	72
44	S3aS4aS5bS6b	48	1.6	73.6
45	S3aS4aS5bS7b	48	1.6	75.2
46	S3aS4aS5bS8b	48	1.6	76.8
47	S3aS5bD7	48	1.6	78.4
48	S3aS5bD8	48	1.6	80
49	S3aS5bS7aS8b	48	1.6	81.6
50	S3bD6S8a	48	1.6	83.2
51	S3bS4aS5bS8a	96	3.2	86.4
52	S3bS5aD8	48	1.6	88
53	S3bS6aS7bS8a	48	1.6	89.6
54	S4aD5S6b	48	1.6	91.2
55	S4aS5bD7	48	1.6	92.8
56	S4aS5bS6aS7b	48	1.6	94.4
57	S4aS5bS6aS8b	48	1.6	96
58	S4bS5aS6bS7a	48	1.6	97.6
59	S4bS5bS7aS8a	24	0.8	98.4
60	S5aS6bS7bS8a	48	1.6	100

6.2. Rater Profiling

We developed a systematic coding scheme to profile the essay-rater distribution process (also noted rater design). Specifically, we assigned a markup label to each subdivided data set. Each markup label is represented by an alphanumeric code. Each code comprises multiple segments of information. A capital character signifies the head of a segment. For instance, the example "S1aS2bS3bS5a" for data subset #13 in Table 23 is composed of four segments (the head of each segment is underlined). What does a segment tell us? A segment is an indicator of a rating produced by a rater. Specifically, it contains three chunks of information, namely the *number of essays graded by a rater for an examinee group* (NESGRE), the *rater identification* (RID), and the *essay identification* (EID). The first segment in the above example "S1a" indicates that rater number 1 scored only the first essay, among the two responded by examinees. The following is a decomposition of the first segment "S1a".

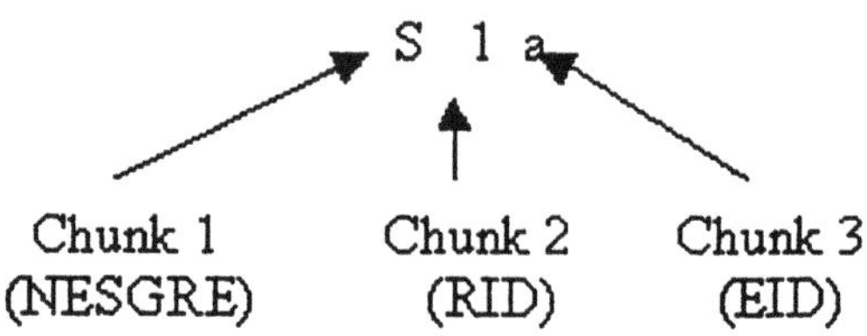

The character *S*, the number *1*, and the character *a* comprise the first, second, and third chunks, respectively. The character *S*, in the above example, stands for "single." More specifically, it reveals that rater 1 (as shown in the second chunk) provided "single" scoring to examinees (i.e., scored only one essay per examinee). Which one of the two essays did rater 1 score? The answer appears in the third chunk, which shows that it was the first essay (denoted by "a") that was graded by rater 1. By the same token, the second segment "S2b" in the markup label "S1aS2bS3bS5a" can be divided into three chunks, namely "S", "2", and "b", with the following interpretations.

(a) Rater 2 was involved in the scoring process (second chunk);
(b) Rater 2 scored only one essay per examinee (first chunk); and
(c) Rater 2 scored essay "b" (third chunk).

Continued to applying the same rule to the rest of the segments ("S3b" and "S5a") in the markup label "S1aS2bS3bS5a", we can learn that raters three and five were also involved in the scoring process (indicated by "3" and "5"); they both scored one essay per examinee (indicated by the last two "Ss" in the markup label); and rater 3 scored the second essay ("3b") whereas rater 5 scored the first essay ("5a"). Note we referred essays "a" and "b" as the first and second essays, respectively. Such a sequential labeling system indicates the order in which essays were developed in the test development stage. The system, however, does not entail the order of essay given to examinees because test administers may counterbalance the order effect of the essays (Kolen and Brennan, 1995).

Combining the information supplied by the all the segments in a markup label, we have a meaningful description for the rater group "S1aS2bS3bS5a" — it is composed of four raters and each of these raters scored only one essay for the examinees assigned to them. More specifically, rater pair 1 and 5 scored the first essay and rater pair 2 and 3 scored the second essay. The following figure depicts how we decomposed the markup label into a meaningful interpretation with four segments of three chunks.

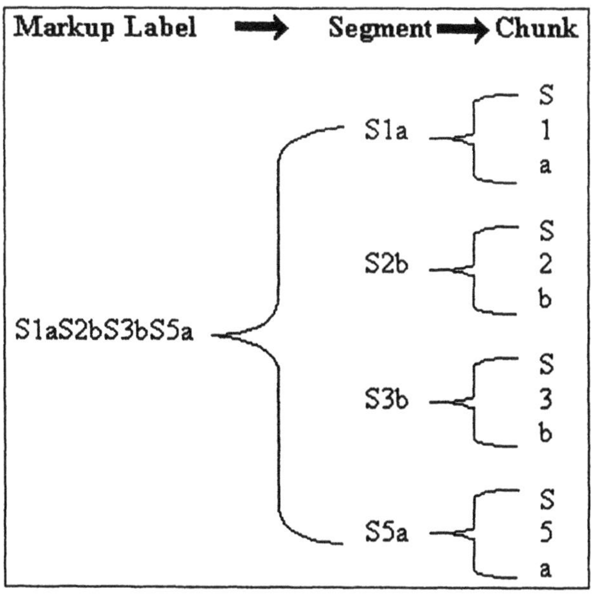

Figure 42: Profile of a rater group.

6.2.1. General Rules for Profiling Raters

By and large, four rules can be used to develop a rater profile or to interpret any markup labels.

Rule 1: A markup label has three segments.

Rule 2: Each segment has three chunks. The first two chunks always appear, whereas the last chunk may not. For instance, when a rater scores all essays for examinees, the essay ID is suppressed because of its redundancy. For instance, we know in the markup label "D1D3" that raters 1 and 3 scored all essays and therefore it is redundant to list all rater IDs.

Rule 3: The first chunk always uses an uppercase character, the second chunk a numerical value, and the third chunk a lowercase character. Alternating the case of the first and last chunks makes a clear distinction among the segments in a markup label.

Rule 4: By counting the number of segments in a markup label, one can determine the structural design of a data subset. For instance, the *crossed* design has only two segments (e.g., D1D3); the *nested* four (e.g., S1aS2bS3bS5a); and the *Modified Balanced Incomplete Block* design (MBIB) three (e.g., D1S4aS7b).

The following are two examples. There are two segments in the markup label "D1D3" ("D1" and "D3"). The first segment ("D1") indicates that rater 1 is a double rater, who scored two essays per examinee. So is rater 2, as indicated in the second segment ("D3"). Since the two raters scored both essays, the two segments had only two chunks. The markup label "D1S4aS7b" contains three segments, namely "D1", "S4a", and "S7b." The first segment shows that rater 1 scored both essays per examinee. The second segment ("S4a") indicates that rater 4 scored only one essay (first essay) per examinee. As shown by the third segment ("S7b"), rater 7 also scored only one essay per examinee ("S"). However, unlike rater 4, rater 7 scored the second essay, as denoted by the third chunk ("b").

In summary, by using the three-chunk notation, the rater profiling system discussed above can accommodate infinite many raters, examinees, and essays. For example, when an assessment has three essays, we can use the character "c" to represent the third essay. It is also flexible enough to annotate any missing data patterns, with each examinee responding to a differential number of essay and each essay receiving differential number of ratings. Moreover, the rater profiling system can be used not only in the Generalizability theory but also in other frameworks such as the Item Response Theory in which hierarchical models are commonly employed (Junker, 2001).

6.2.2. Summary of the Subdividing Program

By contrasting the results of Examples 1 and 2 (Table 21 and Table 22), one can observe that given the same number of raters and examinees, different rater-essay distribution process led to different number of data subsets for analyses. The ability to understand the rater-essay distribution process can shed lights in planning or monitoring the scoring procedures, which are critical in comparing rater performance. Though it is desirable to monitor the distribution process, tracking and reporting the process is a challenging task because of the massive amounts of data in large-scale assessments. The *Subdividing Program* overcomes this computational intensive task by automating the complex process using SPSS. It also produces: (a) a rater design profile to diagnose the distribution process; (b) a summary of the workload of the raters, and (c) a table of estimates of measurement errors for each rater group.

6.3. USING MULTIPLE COMPUTERS TO CONDUCT LARGE-SCALE SIMULATIONS

Computer simulations can be time consuming. The study described in the chapter involved millions of variance component analyses. We had 176 conditions in the simulation study. Each condition was replicated 100 times and each replication required multiple variance component analyses (e.g., the 6000-examinee-28-rater condition required over one hundred data subsets). As a result, over two million analyses were conducted. To run the analyses in a timely fashion, we utilized simultaneously more than 30 computers in public labs of a State University. With this divide-and-conquer approach, all the analyses were conducted within a month of CPU time. The following paragraphs introduce two computer programs developed based on the divide-and-conquer protocol and can be used for any simulation studies.

The *Internet Data Collection Program* allows users to retrieve an SPSS syntax file from a remote computer, select desirable sections of codes in the syntax file, use the codes to run a simulation, collect the simulated data, and send the results back to the remote computer. The *File Merger* allows users to merge an unlimited number of SPSS data files into one large file for subsequent analyses. It automates the file merging process by prompting the user to supply only the file name of any data file to be merged. These two programs are suitable for collecting large amounts of simulated data in a timely fashion and they are discussed more thoroughly in the current sections.

6.3.1. Internet Data Collection Program

The *Internet Data Collection Program* is a standalone program developed in Visual Basic. Prior to using the program, one must develop a syntax file in SPSS format and save the syntax file in an Internet server that supports the File Transfer Protocol (FTP) function. Once the syntax file is prepared, one can go directly to a computer lab and execute the entire simulation process with only a few mouse-clicks.

Prior to the development of the program, the per-computer-setup time required at least two minutes and the research personnel had to manually perform a sequence of repetitious procedures (e.g., typing in the FTP address, creating file directories to save the simulated data, activate SPSS, and select the appropriate sections of syntax). With the program, the per-computer-setup time reduced to lower than 30 seconds. Flexibility is as important as the setup time. Without the program, one has to predetermine a fixed set of experimental conditions for each computer (see Chapter 3 for all the conditions in the current study). For example, computer #1 runs the first 10 experimental conditions; computer #2 runs the second 10 conditions. However, the program relaxes such constraint and thus enables the research personnel to change or select the conditions shortly before the simulation process. This flexibility has many benefits. It is the author's experience that some computers run more quickly than the others even with the same hardware and configurations. Being able to change the simulation conditions can allow the research personnel to better allocate the computational time (e.g., assign more conditions to faster computers). As shown in Figure 43, research personnel can determine the experimental conditions and type them in to Box 3 denoted "Condition ID."

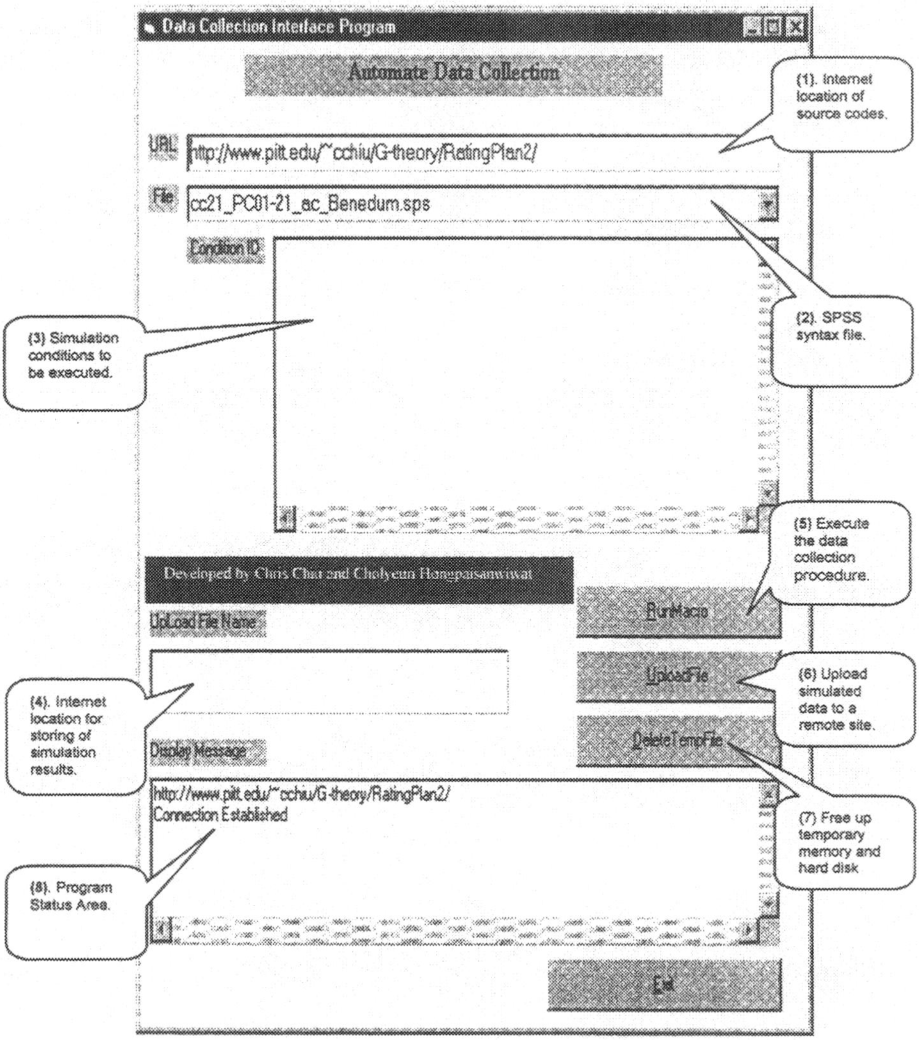

Figure 43: The Internet Data Collection program.

6.3.2. The File Merger Program

The *File Merger*, an add-on program to SPSS, allows users to merge an unlimited number of SPSS data files into one large file for subsequent analyses. It automates the file merging process by prompting the user to supply only one file name of any data file to be merged. It saves the time to specify the name of files. The *File Merger* is particularly useful after data were collected from multiple computers using the *Internet Data Collection Program*. Figure 44 shows the interface of the *File Merger*.

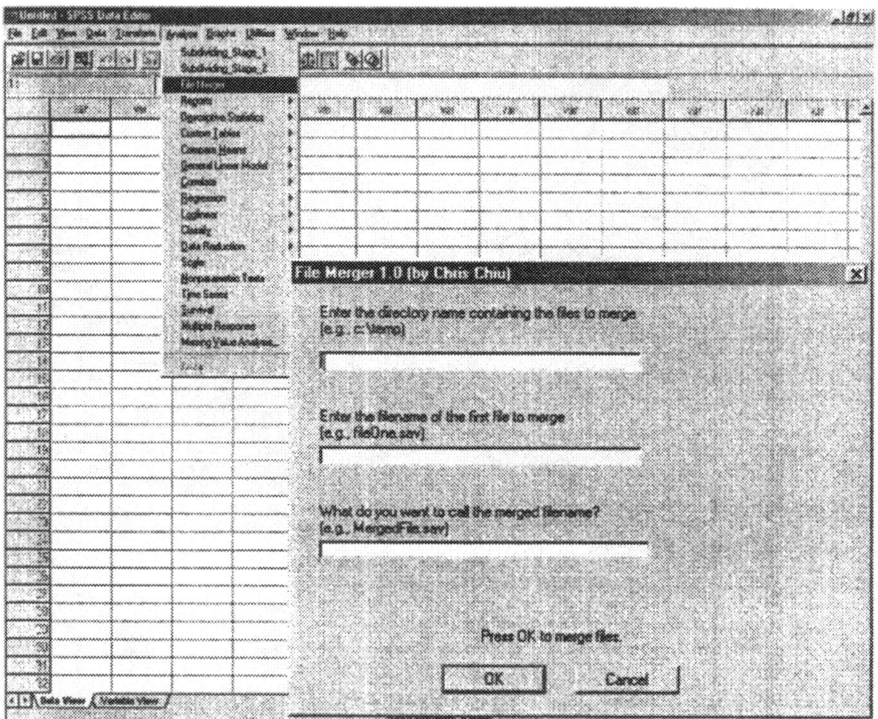

Figure 44: The File Merger program.

6.3.3. Availability

Inquiries for the computer programs can be sent to Chris Chiu (cchiu@pitt.edu), Room 5A24, Posvar Hall, Program in Research Methodology, School of Education, University of Pittsburgh, Pittsburgh, PA 15260. The programs and corresponding documentations are available commercially.

APPENDICES

Appendix A

Equations for scores and coefficients in generalizability theory (Adapted from Brennan, 1992)

G Study

$$\begin{aligned}
X_{pir} = {} & \mu && \text{(grand mean)} \\
& + (\mu_p - \mu) && \text{(person effect)} \\
& + (\mu_i - \mu) && \text{(item effect)} \\
& + (\mu_r - \mu) && \text{(rater effect)} \\
& + (\mu_{pi} - \mu_p - \mu_i + \mu) && \text{(person-by-item interaction)} \\
& + (\mu_{pr} - \mu_p - \mu_r + \mu) && \text{(person-by-rater interaction)} \\
& + (\mu_{ir} - \mu_i - \mu_r + \mu) && \text{(rater x item interaction)} \\
& + (X_{pir} - \mu_{pi} - \mu_{pr} - \mu_{ir} + \mu_p + \mu_i + \mu_r - \mu) && \text{(residual)}
\end{aligned} \tag{27}$$

$$\sigma^2(X_{pir}) = \sigma^2_p + \sigma^2_i + \sigma^2_r + \sigma^2_{pi} + \sigma^2_{pr} + \sigma^2_{ir} + \sigma^2_{pir,e} \tag{28}$$

D Study

$$\text{Relative Error Variance} = \sigma^2_\delta = \frac{\sigma^2_{pi}}{n'_i} + \frac{\sigma^2_{pr}}{n'_r} + \frac{\sigma^2_{pir,e}}{n'_i n'_r} \tag{29}$$

$$\text{Absolute Error Variance} = \sigma^2_\Delta = \frac{\sigma^2_i}{n'_i} + \frac{\sigma^2_r}{n'_r} + \frac{\sigma^2_{ir}}{n'_i n'_r} + \frac{\sigma^2_{pi}}{n'_i} + \frac{\sigma^2_{pr}}{n'_r} + \frac{\sigma^2_{pir,e}}{n'_i n'_r} \tag{30}$$

$$\text{Generalizability Coefficient} = \rho^2 = \frac{\sigma_p^2}{\sigma_p^2 + \sigma_\delta^2} \tag{31}$$

$$\text{Dependability Coefficient} = \Phi = \frac{\sigma_p^2}{\sigma_p^2 + \sigma_\Delta^2} \tag{32}$$

$$\text{Standard Error of Measurement} = \text{SEM} = \sqrt{\sigma_\Delta^2} \tag{33}$$

Appendix B

Standard error for variance components in a two facet crossed design[2]

$$\sigma(\hat{\sigma}_p^2) = \left[2\frac{(\hat{\sigma}^2_{pir,e} + n_i * \hat{\sigma}^2_{pi} + n_r * \hat{\sigma}^2_{pi} + * n_r * \hat{\sigma}^2_p)^2}{(n_p+1) * n_i^2 * n_r^2} + 2\frac{(\hat{\sigma}^2_{pir,e} + n_r * \hat{\sigma}^2_{pi})^2}{((n_p-1) * (n_i-1)+2) * n_i^2 * n_r^2} + 2\frac{(\hat{\sigma}^2_{pir,e} + n_i * \hat{\sigma}^2_{pr})^2}{((n_p-1) * (n_r-1)+2) * n_i^2 * n_r^2} + 2\frac{(\hat{\sigma}^2_{pir,e})^2}{((n_p-1) * (n_i-1) * (n_r-1)+2) * n_i^2 * n_r^2} \right]^{\frac{1}{2}} \quad (34)$$

$$\sigma(\hat{\sigma}_i^2) = \left[2\frac{(\hat{\sigma}^2_{pir,e} + n_p * \hat{\sigma}^2_{ir} + n_r * \hat{\sigma}^2_{pi} + * n_p * n_r * \hat{\sigma}^2_i)^2}{(n_i+1) * n_p^2 * n_r^2} + 2\frac{(\hat{\sigma}^2_{pir,e} + n_r * \hat{\sigma}^2_{pi})^2}{((n_p-1) * (n_i-1)+2) * n_p^2 * n_r^2} + 2\frac{(\hat{\sigma}^2_{pir,e} + n_p * \hat{\sigma}^2_{ir})^2}{((n_i-1) * (n_r-1)+2) * n_p^2 * n_r^2} + 2\frac{(\hat{\sigma}^2_{pir,e})^2}{((n_p-1) * (n_i-1) * (n_r-1)+2) * n_p^2 * n_r^2} \right]^{\frac{1}{2}} \quad (35)$$

$$\sigma(\hat{\sigma}_r^2) = \left[2\frac{(\hat{\sigma}^2_{pir,e} + n_p * \hat{\sigma}^2_{ir} + n_i * \hat{\sigma}^2_{pr} + * n_p n_i * \hat{\sigma}^2_r)^2}{(n_r+1) * n_i^2 * n_p^2} + 2\frac{(\hat{\sigma}^2_{pir,e} + n_i * \hat{\sigma}^2_{pr})^2}{((n_p-1) * (n_r-1)+2) * n_i^2 * n_p^2} + 2\frac{(\hat{\sigma}^2_{pir,e} + n_p * \hat{\sigma}^2_{ir})^2}{((n_i-1) * (n_r-1)+2) * n_i^2 * n_p^2} + 2\frac{(\hat{\sigma}^2_{pir,e})^2}{((n_p-1) * (n_i-1) * (n_r-1)+2) * n_i^2 * n_p^2} \right]^{\frac{1}{2}} \quad (36)$$

$$\sigma(\hat{\sigma}_{pi}^2) = \left[2\frac{(\hat{\sigma}^2_{pir,e} + n_r * \hat{\sigma}^2_{pi})^2}{((n_p-1) * (n_i-1)+2) * n_r^2} + 2\frac{(\hat{\sigma}^2_{pir,e})^2}{((n_p-1) * (n_i-1)(n_r-1)+2) * n_r^2} \right]^{\frac{1}{2}} \quad (37)$$

---

[2] Equations for the standard errors were derived by substituting variance components, sample sizes, and mean squares into the general formula reported in Brennen (1992, p. 101, 6.2.1).

$$\sigma(\hat{\sigma}^2_{pr}) = \left[2\frac{(\hat{\sigma}^2_{pir,e}+n_i{*}\hat{\sigma}^2_{pr})^2}{((n_p-1){*}(n_r-1)+2){*}n_i{}^2} + 2\frac{(\hat{\sigma}^2_{pir,e})^2}{((n_p-1){*}(n_i-1)(n_r-1)+2){*}n_i{}^2} \right]^{\frac{1}{2}}$$

(38)

$$\sigma(\hat{\sigma}^2_{ir}) = \left[2\frac{(\hat{\sigma}^2_{pir,e}+n_p{*}\hat{\sigma}^2_{ir})^2}{((n_p-1){*}(n_r-1)+2){*}n_p{}^2} + 2\frac{(\hat{\sigma}^2_{pir,e})^2}{((n_p-1){*}(n_i-1)(n_r-1)+2){*}n_p{}^2} \right]^{\frac{1}{2}}$$

(39)

$$\sigma(\hat{\sigma}^2_{pir,e}) = \left[2\frac{(\hat{\sigma}^2_{pir,e})^2}{(n_p-1){*}(n_i-1)(n_r-1)+2} \right]^{\frac{1}{2}}$$

(40)

Appendix C

Computation of misclassification rate for conjunctive decision rules

Misclassification Rate (Probability of Downward Misclassifications as a Function of the SEM):

= 1 - Correct Classification Rate

= 1 - {P(passing item 1 | SEM) ***X*** P(passing item 2 | SEM) ***X*** ... ***X*** P(passing item # *i* | SEM)}

= 1 - {[1 - P(failing item 1 | SEM)] ***X*** [1 - P(failing item 2 | SEM)] ***X*** ... ***X*** [1 - P(failing item i | SEM)]

Example (Cronbach et al., 1997, p. 381):

Question: Assuming a hypothetical examinee had universe scores of (2.5, 2.5, 2.5), (3.5, 3.5, 3.5) and the absolute standard error of measurement (SEM) of a measurement procedure is 0.7, what is the chance that the examinee had one or more scores less than 1.5?

Answer:

$= 1-[\ \{1-P(Z < -(2.5-1.5)/.7)\}^3 \text{ x } \{1-P(Z < -(3.5-1.5)/.7)\}^3]$

= .24

~ 25%

Appendix D

Illustration of an out-of-range sample correlation based on different data sets for sample covariance and variances

Case	**Variable A**	**Variable B**
1	*1*	*1*
2	*2*	*2*
3	5	.
4	5	.
5	.	5
6	*10*	*10*

Note: σ_a and σ_b are based on 5 and 4 data points, respectively. σ_{ab} is based on only 3 cases that are italicized. The correlation $r_{ab} = \sigma_{ab}/(\sigma_a * \sigma_b) = 1.14$.

Appendix E

Correlations based on missing data

Y_1	1	2	3	4	1	2	3	4	-	-	-	-
Y_2	1	2	3	4	-	-	-	-	1	2	3	4
Y_3	-	-	-	-	1	2	3	4	4	3	2	1

Note: r12=1, r13=1, r23=-1. Source: Little & Rubin (1987, p.43).

Appendix F

The structure of a *Modified Balanced Incomplete Block* Design

The *MBIB*, a variation of the balanced incomplete block design (BIB) (e.g., Montgomery, 1997, p.208; Searle et al., 1992, p.5), is a balanced design because every examinee receives two ratings on both essays. The incompleteness comes into play due to the fact that one reader grades the essay twice and yet the two other different raters grade the essay only once. The *MBIB* design is specially designed for situations differing from the BIB design that the *MBIB* design has an additional factor to the BIB design. As can be seen in

Figure 45 there are two levels in the item factors (items 1 and 2). As can be observed in Figure 45 a data subset with the *MBIB* design using raters A, B, and C, with A being the rater assign scores to both items, can have $n_{p,3,1}$ examinees. The first subscript p indicates that the sample size n refers to the number of examinees. The second subscript 3 indicates that the data set exhibits a *MBIB* design and the third subscript 1 indicates that the data set is the first set in the *MBIB* design. The total number of cases that can be analyzed by the *MBIB* model is $n_{p,3,\cdot} = \sum_{s=1}^{S_t} n_{p,3,s}$. The entire sparsely filled data has a total number of cases of $N = \sum_{t=1}^{3}\sum_{s=11}^{S_t} n_{p,t,s}$.

Examinee	Item 1 Rater A	Item 1 Rater B	Item 1 Rater C	Item 2 Rater A	Item 2 Rater B	Item 2 Rater C
1	$X_{3,1,1,1,A}$	$X_{3,1,1,1,B}$		$X_{3,1,1,2,A}$		$X_{3,1,1,2,C}$
2	$X_{3,2,1,1,A}$		$X_{3,2,1,1,C}$		$X_{3,2,1,2,B}$	$X_{3,2,1,2,C}$
3		$X_{3,3,1,1,B}$	$X_{3,3,1,1,C}$	$X_{3,3,1,2,A}$	$X_{3,3,1,2,B}$	
4	$X_{3,4,1,1,A}$	$X_{3,4,1,1,B}$			$X_{3,4,1,2,B}$	$X_{3,41,2,C}$
5	$X_{3,5,1,1,A}$		$X_{3,5,1,1,C}$	$X_{3,5,1,2,A}$	$X_{3,5,1,2,B}$	
6		$X_{3,6,1,1,B}$	$X_{3,6,1,1,C}$	$X_{3,6,1,2,A}$		$X_{3,6,1,2,C}$
	⋮	⋮	⋮	⋮	⋮	⋮
m	$X_{3,St,np,2,\bullet,1,A}$	$X_{3,St,np,2,\bullet,1,B}$			$X_{3,St,np,2,\bullet,2,B}$	$X_{3,St,np,2,\bullet,2,C}$

Note: The Xs indicate scores assigned to an essay. The subscripts indicate the location of the score, where location is defined as the structural design (first subscript), data subset (second subscript), examinee (third subscript), item (fourth subscript), and rater (fifth subscript) for the corresponding score.

Figure 45: Hypothetical data subsets for the MBIB design.

Appendix G

A mathematical model to determine the size of a rater pool.

To figure the number of raters needed for the entire scoring procedure, we first develop a simple mathematical model. Equation (41) gives a generic model where the number of raters needed is determined by two quantities, namely the total number of ratings in an administration of a test (denoted *Total workload in minutes*) and the total amount of time, in minutes, that an average rater can put in during the entire scoring procedure (denoted *Total work time per rater*).

$$Number\_of\_raters\_needed = Total\_workload\_in\_minutes \,/\, Total\_work\_time\_per\_rater \qquad (41)$$

As can be observed, more raters are needed as the total workload increases while holding the total work time per rater constant. By the same token, fewer raters are needed as the total workload decreases.

We now define more specifically *Total workload in minutes* and *Total work time per rater* in terms of other practical constraints such as the available time for generating and reporting the scores. By defining those two quantities as a function of other practical constraints, we will be able to decide how many raters are needed given the available resources (e.g., how much time do we have until the scores must be analyzed and reported?). The definitions of those two quantities can be modified to accommodate constraints of individual scoring centers. In addition, the values of those two quantities can vary from one administration to the others within an individual scoring center, depending upon policy, needs, and available resources. In the examples that follow, we define the total workload and total work time in terms of constraints common to essay scoring, according to anecdotal reports. Thus,

$$Total\_workload\_in\_minutes = n\_examinees \; X \; n\_essays\_answered\_by\_an\_examinee \; X \; n\_ratings\_per\_essay \; X \; reading\_time\_per\_essay\_in\_minutes, \qquad (42)$$

$$Total\_work\_time\_per\_rater = n\_total\_scoring\_days \; X \; n\_work\_hours\_per\_rater\_per\_day \; X \; 60\_minutes. \qquad (43)$$

By substituting values into Equations (42) and (43) into (41), we reach the following symbolic equation.

$$\text{Number of raters needed} = \frac{n_{p..} \bullet n_{i..} \bullet n_{r/e} \bullet t_e}{n_d \bullet n_h \bullet 60}, \qquad (44)$$

where $n_{p..}$ = number of examinees,

$n_{i..}$ = number of items (essays) responded to by an examinee,

$n_{r/e}$ = number of ratings on each essay,

t_e = average time needed to score an essay by a rater (in minute),

n_d = number of days available to complete scoring, and

n_h = average work hours per day by a rater.

For instance, let us assume 6,000 examinees took a test and each examinee responded to two 500-word writing prompts. Two different raters score each writing prompt. We further assume that it takes an average of 10 minutes for a reading of an essay. Substituting this information into Equation (44), we need 14 raters to complete the scoring in 40 workdays of 7.5 hours ((6000*2*2*10)/(40*7.5*60) = 13.3).

Appendix H

A multivariate regression model predicting the accuracy of variance components.

Table 24: Wilks' Lamda for predicting accuracy of variance components

Multivariate Tests (Wilks' Lamda)					
Effect	Value	F	Hypothesis df	Error df	p-values
Intercept	0.006	204499.176	7	8788	0.000
N_P	1.000	0.440	7	8788	0.877
N_R	1.000	0.543	7	8788	0.802
VAR_I	0.999	0.869	7	8788	0.530
VAR_PR	1.000	0.439	7	8788	0.878
MIN_BAT	1.000	0.602	7	8788	0.755

Note: N_P refers to the sample size of examinees (levels sampled 750, 1500, 3000, and 6000)
N_R refers to the size of rater pools (level tested sampled 2, 4, 8, 14, and 28)
VAR_I refers to the magnitude of the item effect (levels sampled included 0.02 and 0.11)
VAR_R refers to the magnitude of the person by rater effect (levels sampled included 0.01 and 0.1)
MIN_BAT refers to the minimum batch size imposed to data subsets (levels sampled included 12 and 24)

Table 25: Regression models for the accuracy of the variance components in the *disconnected crossed* rating plan

Dependent Variable (Accuracy)	Predictors	Coefficients	Std. Error	t	Sig.
Person[a]	*Intercept*	1.00	0.003	364.652	0.000
	N_P	0.00	0.000	0.953	0.341
	N_R	0.00	0.000	-0.291	0.771
	VAR_I	-0.01	0.015	-0.747	0.455
	VAR_PR	0.01	0.015	0.616	0.538
	MIN_BAT	0.00	0.000	-1.591	0.112
Item[a]	*Intercept*	1.00	0.064	15.739	0.000
	N_P	0.00	0.000	-1.100	0.271
	N_R	0.00	0.003	-0.977	0.329
	VAR_I	0.09	0.356	0.264	0.792
	VAR_PR	-0.08	0.356	-0.214	0.831
	MIN_BAT	0.00	0.003	1.027	0.305
Rater[b]	*Intercept*	0.96	0.053	17.921	0.000
	N_P	0.00	0.000	0.633	0.527
	N_R	0.00	0.002	0.002	0.999
	VAR_I	0.24	0.298	0.791	0.429
	VAR_PR	-0.10	0.298	-0.319	0.750
	MIN_BAT	0.00	0.002	0.221	0.825
Person by Item[a]	*Intercept*	1.00	0.002	472.431	0.000
	N_P	0.00	0.000	-0.306	0.760
	N_R	0.00	0.000	-1.134	0.257
	VAR_I	-0.01	0.012	-1.023	0.306
	VAR_PR	-0.02	0.012	-1.273	0.203
	MIN_BAT	0.00	0.000	0.990	0.322
Person by Rater[b]	*Intercept*	1.00	0.016	61.034	0.000
	N_P	0.00	0.000	-0.845	0.398
	N_R	0.00	0.001	0.322	0.748
	VAR_I	0.00	0.092	-0.030	0.976
	VAR_PR	-0.07	0.092	-0.718	0.473
	MIN_BAT	0.00	0.001	0.563	0.573
Item by Rater[b]	*Intercept*	0.99	0.034	28.937	0.000
	N_P	0.00	0.000	-0.106	0.916
	N_R	0.00	0.001	-0.033	0.973
	VAR_I	0.20	0.192	1.027	0.304
	VAR_PR	-0.04	0.192	-0.201	0.840
	MIN_BAT	0.00	0.001	0.227	0.820
Person by Item by Rater[b]	*Intercept*	1.00	0.002	656.061	0.000
	N_P	0.00	0.000	0.555	0.579
	N_R	0.00	0.000	0.860	0.390
	VAR_I	-0.01	0.009	-0.589	0.556
	VAR_PR	0.00	0.009	-0.222	0.824
	MIN_BAT	0.00	0.000	-0.715	0.475

Note: N_P refers to the sample size of examinees (levels sampled 750, 1500, 3000, and 6000)
N_R refers to the size of rater pools (level tested sampled 2, 4, 8, 14, and 28)
VAR_I refers to the magnitude of the item effect (levels sampled included 0.02 and 0.11)
VAR_R refers to the magnitude of the person by rater effect (levels sampled included 0.01 and 0.1)
MIN_BAT refers to the minimum batch size imposed to data subsets (levels sampled included 12 and 24)
a: R Squared = .001 (Adjusted R Squared = .000)
b: R Squared = .000 (Adjusted R Squared = .000)

REFERENCES

Aczel, A. D. (1996). *Complete business statistics.* (3rd ed.). Chicago: Irwin.

Alan, G., and Liu, J. (1981). *Computer Solution of Large Sparse Positive Definite Systems,* Prentice-Hall.

Authors. (1996). *The NAEP Guide: How Does NAEP Reliably Score and Process Millions of Student-Composed Responses?* (Technical Report Number 97-990). Tempa, Florida: National Center for Educational Statistics (NCES).

Authors. (1998a). *Collegiate Assessment of Academic Proficiency (CAAP)* (Internet Web Wide Web Document). Iowa City, Iowa: ACT, Inc.

Authors. (1998b). *Test of English as a Foreign Language (TOEFL): Test of written English online* (Internet World Wide Web Document). Princeton, NJ: ETS.

Babb, J. S. (1986). *Pooling maximum likelihood estimates of variance components obtained from subsets of unbalanced data.* Master's thesis. Cornell University.

Bejar, I. I. (1993). A generative approach to psychological and educational measurement. In R. J. Mislevy, I. I. Bejar, and N. Frederiksen (Ed.), *Test theory for a new generation of tests.* (pp. 323-357): Lawrence Erlbaum Associates, Inc, Hillsdale, NJ.

Bejar, I. I. (1999, July). *The future of scoring open-ended assessments.* Personal Communication. Educational Testing Service.

Bell, J. F. (1985). Generalizability theory: The software problem. *Journal of Educational Statistics, 10*(1), 19-29.

Bennett, R. E. (2001). How the Internet Will Help Large-Scale Assessment Reinvent Itself. *Education Policy Analysis Archives,* 9(5).

Bracey, G. W. (1987). Measurement-driven instruction: Catchy phrase, dangerous practice. *Phi Delta Kappan, 68,* 683-686.

Brennan, R. L. (1992). *Elements of generalizability theory.* Iowa City: American College Testing.

Brennan, R. L. (1997). A perspective on the history of generalizability theory. *Educational Measurement: Issues and Practice, 16*(4), 14-20.

Brennan, R. L. (1998). Misconceptions at the intersection of measurement theory and practice. *Educational Measurement: Issues and Practice* 17(1): 5-9.

Brennan, R. L., Gao, X., & Colton, D. A. (1995). Generalizability analyses of Work Keys listening and writing tests. *Educational and Psychological Measurement, 55*(2), 157-176.

Brennan, R. L., Jarjoura, D., & Deaton, E. L. (1980). *Some issues concerning the estimation and interpretation of variance components in generalizability theory* (Technical Bulletin 36). Iowa City, Iowa: ACT.

Brennan, R. L., & Kane, M. T. (1977). An index of dependability for mastery tests. *Journal of Educational Measurement, 14*, 277-289.

Brennan, R. L. (2000). Generalizability theory and performance assessment. *Applied Psychological Measurement*, 24(4), 339-353.

Burdick, R. K. & F. A. Graybill (1992). *Confidence Intervals on Variance Components.* New York, Marcel Dekker.

Chiu, C. W. T., & Wolfe, E. W. (1997, April). *Generalizability Theory: A New Approach to Analyze Non-Crossed Performance Assessment Data.* Paper presented at the American Educational Research Association annual meeting, Chicago, IL.

Chiu, C. W. T., & Wolfe, E. W. (in press). A method for analyzing sparse data matrices in the Generalizability theory framework. *Applied Psychological Measurement.*

Clauser, B. E., Clyman, S. G., & Swanson, D. B. (1999). Components of rater error in a complex performance assessment. *Journal of Educational Measurement, 36*(1), 29-45.

Clauser, B. E., Swanson, D. B., & Clyman, S. G. (1996). The generalizability of scores from a performance of physicians' patient management skills. *Academic Medicine (RIME Supplement), 71*, S109-111.

Crocker, L., & Algina, J. (1986). Reliability and the Classical True Score Model. In L. Crocker & J. Algina (Eds.), *Introduction to Classical and Modern Test Theory* (pp. 105-130). New York, NY: Rinehart and Winston.

Cronbach, L. J., Bradburn, N. M., and Horvitz, D. G. (1994). *Sampling and statistical procedures used in the California Learning Assessment System. Report of the Select Committee.*

Cronbach, L. J., Gleser, G. C., Nanda, H., & Rajaratnam, N. (1972). *The dependability of behavioral measurements: Theory of generalizability for scores and profiles.* New York: Wiley.

Cronbach, L. J., Linn, R. L., Brennan, R. L., & Haertel, E. H. (1997). Generalizability analysis for performance assessments of student achievement or school effectiveness. *Educational and Psychological Measurement, 57*(3), 373-399.

Donoghue, J. R. and Hombo, C. M. (2000). *A Comparison of Different Model Assumptions bout Rater Effects.* the Annual Meeting of the National Council on Measurement in Education, New Orleans, LA.

Engelhard, G., Jr. (1997). Constructing rater and task banks for performance assessments. *Journal of Outcome Measurement, 1*(1), 19-93.

Fleiss, J. L. (1981). Balanced incomplete block designs for inter-rater reliability studies. *Applied Psychological Measurement 5*, 105-112.

Giesbrecht, F. G. (1983). An efficient procedure for computing MINQUE of variance components and generalized least squares estimates of fixed effects. *Communications in Statistics, Series A: Theory and Method, 12*, 2169-2177.

Goodnight, J. H. (1978). *Computing MIVQUE0 Estimates of Variance Components* (SAS Techincal Report R-105). Cary, NC: SAS Institute.

Gordon, B. (1998, Sep). *Scoring performance assessment.* Personal Communication. University of Georgia.

Hamilton, L., C. (1992). *Regression with Graphics*. Belmont, CA: Duxbury Press.

Harwell, M. (1992). Summarizing Monte Carlo results in methodological research. *Applied Psychology Measurement, 17*(4), 297-313.

Harwell, M., Stone, C. A., Hsu, T. C., & Kirisci, L. (1996). Monte Carlo studies in item response theory. *Applied Psychology Measurement, 20*(2), 101-125.

Hays, W. L., & Winkler, R. L. (1970). *Statistics: Probability, inference, and decision.* (Vol. II). New York: Holt, Rinehart and Winston, Inc.

Hedges, L. V., & Olkin, I. (1985). *Statistical methods for Meta-Analysis*. New York: Academic Press.

Henderson, C. R. (1953). Estimation of variance and covariance components. *Biometrics, 9*, 226-252.

Hombo, C. (1999, July). *The potential of electronic raters to score national assessments.* Personal Communication. Educational Testing Service.

Hoyt, W. T. (2000). Rater bias in psychological research: When is it a problem and what can we do about it? *Psychological Methods*. 5(1), 64-86.

Junker, B. (2001). On the interplay between nonparametric and parametric IRT, with some thoughts about the future. (pp. 247-276). In *Essays on Item Response Theory.* New York: Springer-Verlag.

Kalaian, H. A., & Becker, B. J. (1996). *Modeling differences in variability.* Paper presented at the Annual Meeting of the American Educational Research Association, San Diego, CA.

Kane, M. T. (1982). A sampling model for validity. *Applied Psychological Measurement, 6*, 125-160.

Kane, M. T., Crooks, T., and Cohen, A. (1999). Validating measures of performance. *Educational Measurement: Issues and Practice, 18(2)*, 5-17.

Kim, J. O., & Curry, J. (1977). The treatment of missing data in multivariate analysis. *Social Methodological Research, 6*, 215-240.

Kolen, M. J., & Brennan, R. L. (1995). *Test Equating: Methods and Practices.* New York: Springer.

Koretz, D., Stecher, B., & McCaffrey, D. (1994). The Vermont Portfolio Assessment Program: findings and implications. *Educational Measurement: Issues and Practice, 13*, 5-6.

Lane, S., Liu, M., Ankenmann, R. D., & Stone, C. A. (1996). Generalizability and validity of a Mathematics performance assessment. *Journal of Educational Measurement, 33*(1), 71-92.

Linn, R. L., Burton, E., DeStefano, L., & Hanson, M. (1996). Generalizability of New Standards Project 1993 Pilot Study Tasks in Mathematics. *Applied Measurement in Education, 9*(3), 201-214.

Little, R. J. A., & Rubin, D. B. (1987). *Statistical Analysis with Missing Data.* New York: John Wiley & Sons.

Longford, N. T. (1995). *Models for uncertainty in educational testing.* New York: Spring-Verlag.

Luecht, R. M., Smith, P. L. (1989). *The Effects of Bootstrapping Strategies on the Estimation of Variance Components.* Paper presented at the Annual Meeting of the American Educational Research Association, San Francisco, CA.

Malley, J. D. (1986). *Optimal unbiased estimation of variance components.* (Vol. 39). New York: Springer-Verlay.

Marcoulides, G.A. (1988). *An alternative method for variance component estimation: Applications to generalizability theory.* Unpublished Dissertation. University of California, Los Angeles.

Marcoulides, G. A. (1990). An alternative method for estimating variance components in generalizability theory. *Psychological Reports, 66*, 379-386.

Mehrens, W. A. (1987). Validity issues in tearcher licensure tests. *Journal of Personnel Evaluation in Education, 1*, 195-22.

Mehrens, W. A. (1992). Using performance assessment for accountability purposes. *Educational Measurement: Issues and Practice, 11*(1), 3-9.

Messick, S. (1989). Meaning and values in test validation: The science and ethics of assessment. *Educational Researcher*, 5-11.

Millman, J., & Glass, G. V. (1967). Rules of thumb for writing the ANOVA table. *Journal of Educational Measurement, 4*(2), 41-51.

Montgomery, D. C. (1997). Randomized Blocks, Latin Square, and Related Designs, *Design and Analysis of Experiments* (pp. 208-210). New York, NY: John Wiley & Son, Inc.

Mooney, C. Z. (1997). *Monte Carlo Simulation.* (Vol. no. 116). Thousand Oaks, CA: Sage.

Myford, C. M., Marr, D. B., & Linacre, J. M. (1995). *Reader calibration and its potential role in equating for the Test of Written English* (Report prepared by the Center for Performance Assessment MS # 95-02). Princeton: Educational Testing Service.

Nitko, A. J. (1996). *Educational Assessment of Students.* (2nd ed). New Jersey, NY: Englewood Cliffs.

Olsen, A., Seely, J., & Birkes, D. (1976). Invariant quadratic unbiased estimation for two variance components. *Annals of Statistcs, 4*, 878-890.

Othman, A. R. (1995). *Examining task sampling variability in science performance assessments.* Unpublished Dissertation. University of California, Santa Barbara.

Patterson. P.(1985). *An investigation of the dependability of criterion-referenced test scores using generalizability theory.* Unpublished Dissertation. University of Wisconsin - Madison.

Patz, R. (1996). *Markov Chain Monte Carlo Methods for Item Response Theory Models.* Unpublished Dissertation, Carnegie Mellon University.

Pearson, P.D. (1998). *Aligning standards for teaching: What do we have to gain?* Paper presented at the National Conference on High Standards for Outstanding Achievement in Education: Examining the Issues, E. Lansing, MI.

Psychometrika Editorial Board. (1979). Publication policy regarding Monte Carlo studies. *Psychometrika*, 44(2), 133-4.

Rao, P. S. R. S. (1997). *Variance components estimation: Mixed models, methodologies and applications.* New York, NY: Chapman & Hall.

Rao, P. S. R. S. (1997). Combination information from experiments (pp.147-154) In *Variance components estimation: mixed models, methodologies and applications.* New York, NY: Chapman & Hall.

Raudenbush, S. W. (1988). Estimating change in dispersion. *Journal of Educational Statistics, 13*(2), 148 - 171.

Rencher, A. C. (1995). *Methods of multivariate analysis.* New York: Wiley.

Rubinstein, R. Y. (1981). *Simulation and the Monte Carlo Method.* New York: John Wiley & Sons.

Satterthwaite, F. E. (1941). Synthesis of variance. *Psychometriaka, 6*, 309-16.

Satterthwaite, F. E. (1946). An approximate distribution of estimates of variance components. *Biometrics Bulletin, 2*, 110-114.

Schafer, W. (1998, Sept). *Scoring performance assessments.* Personal Communication. The Maryland School Performance Assessment Program.

Schroeder, M. L. (1986). *Inferential Procedures for Multifaceted Coefficients of Generalizability.* Unpublished Dissertation. The University of British Columbia (CANADA).

Searle, S. R. (1971). Topics in variance component estimation. *Biometrics, 27*, 1-76.

Searle, S. R. (1987). *Linear Models for Unbalanced Data.* New York, NY: John Wiley & Sons.

Searle, S. R., Casella, G., & McCulloch, C. E. (1992). *Variance Components.* New York, NY: Wiley.

Seeger, P. (1970). A method of estimating variance components in unbalanced designs. *Technometrics, 12*(2), 207-218.

Shavelson, R. J., Baxter, G. P., & Gao, X. (1993). Sampling variability of performance assessments. *Journal of Educational Measurement, 30*(3), 215-232.

Shavelson, R. J., & Webb, N. M. (1981). Generalizability theory 1973-1980. *British Journal of Mathematical and Statistical Psychology, 34*, 133-166.

Shavelson, R. J., & Webb, N. M. (1991). *Generalizability theory: A primer.* Newbury Park, CA: Sage.

Smith, P. L. (1978). Sampling errors of variance components in small sample multifacet Generalizability Studies. *Journal of Educational Statistics, 3*(4), 319-346.

Smith, P. L. (1981). Gaining accuracy in generalizability theory: Using multiple designs. *Journal of Educational Measurement, 18*, 147-154.

Smith, P. L. (1982). A confidence interval approach for variance component estimates in the context of generalizability theory. *Educational and Psychological Measurement, 42, 459-466.*

SPSS (2000). *SPSS® 10.0 Developer's Guide. Chicago, IL: Authors.*

Townsend, E. C. (1968). *Unbiased Estimators of Variance Components in Simple Unbalanced Designs.* Unpublished Ph.D. Dissertation, Cornell University, Ithaca, New York.

Tucker, M. (1998, May 5-7). *High Standards for Improved Achievement in Education.* Paper presented at the High Standards for Outstanding Achievement in Education: Examining the Issues, E. Lansing, MI

U.S. Department of Education. (1998b). *Writing Framework and Specifications for the 1998 National Assessment of Educational Progress* (Report). Washington, D.C.: Authors.

Vickers, D. (1998, Sept). *Scoring performance assessments.* Personal Communication. North Carolina Performance Assessment Program.

Wainer, H. (1993). Measurement problems. *Journal of Educational Measurement, 30*(1), 1-21.

Welch, C. (1996, July). *Scoring performance assessments.* Personal Communication. Performance Assessment Center, ACT, Inc.

Wolfe, E. W. (1998, Sept). *Scoring performance assessment.* Personal Communication. University of Florida.

Wolfe, E.W., Chiu, C.W.T., & Myford, C.M. (2000). Detecting rater effects with a multi-faceted Rasch rating scale model. In M. Wilson & G. Engelhard (Eds.), *Objective Measurement: Theory into Practice* (Vol. 5).

Ysseldyke, J., & Olsen, K. (1999). *Putting Alternate Assessments into Practice: What to Measure and Possible Sources of Data.* Synthesis Report No. 28, National Center on Educational Outcomes. [Online] Available http://www.coled.umn.edu/nceo/OnlinePubs/awgfinal.html

Subject Index

F

G

H

I

L

M

N

O

P

Q

R

T

U

V

W

Author Index

A

B

C

D

E

F

G

H

J

K

L

M

N

O

P

R

S

GPSR Compliance
The European Union's (EU) General Product Safety Regulation (GPSR) is a set of rules that requires consumer products to be safe and our obligations to ensure this.

If you have any concerns about our products, you can contact us on

ProductSafety@springernature.com

In case Publisher is established outside the EU, the EU authorized representative is:

Springer Nature Customer Service Center GmbH
Europaplatz 3
69115 Heidelberg, Germany

www.ingramcontent.com/pod-product-compliance
Ingram Content Group UK Ltd.
Pitfield, Milton Keynes, MK11 3LW, UK
UKHW021239300926
15471UKWH00013B/699

* 9 7 8 9 4 0 1 0 0 6 5 1 4 *